BOYHOOD AMONG

THE WOOLIES

BOYHOOD AMONG THE WOOLIES

GROWING UP ON A BASQUE SHEEP RANCH

RICHARD W. ETULAIN

BASALT BOOKS

Pullman, Washington

BASALT BOOKS

Basalt Books
PO Box 645910
Pullman, Washington 99164-5910
Phone: 800-354-7360
Email: basalt.books@wsu.edu
Website: basaltbooks.wsu.edu

First printing 2023, Second printing 2024
Library of Congress Cataloging-in-Publication Data

Names: Etulain, Richard W., author.
Title: Boyhood among the woolies : growing up on a Basque sheep ranch /
    Richard W. Etulain.
Other titles: Growing up on a Basque sheep ranch
Description: Pullman, Washington : Washington State University Press,
    [2023] | Includes bibliographical references and index.
Identifiers: LCCN 2023004278 | ISBN 9781638640073 (paperback) Subjects:
LCSH: Etulain, Richard W.--Childhood and youth. | Etulain family.
    | Ranch life--Washington (State)--Biography. | Basque
    Americans--Washington (State)--Biography. | Sheep ranchers--Washington
    (State)--Adams County--Biography. | Sheep ranches--Washington
    (State)--History--20th century. | Adams County (Wash.)--Biography. |
    BISAC: BIOGRAPHY & AUTOBIOGRAPHY / Personal Memoirs | BIOGRAPHY
&   AUTOBIOGRAPHY / Cultural, Ethnic & Regional / General
Classification: LCC F897.A2 E88 2023 | DDC 979.7/34092
    [B]--dc23/eng/20230203
LC record available at https://lccn.loc.gov/2023004278

Basalt Books is an imprint of Washington State University Press.
The Washington State University Pullman campus is located on the homelands of the Niimíipuu (Nez
Perce) Tribe and the Palus people. We acknowledge their presence here since time immemorial
and recognize their continuing connection to the land, to the water, and to their ancestors. WSU
Press is committed to publishing works that foster a deeper understanding of the Pacific
Northwest and the contributions of its Native peoples.

Cover design by Patrick Brommer.

To the memories of Dad and Mom, warmest wishes

CONTENTS

PREFACE

Three events, several years apart, spurred me on to write this memoir. In the early 1970s as I was preparing a book eventually titled *Conversations with Wallace Stegner on Western History and Literature* (1983), I encountered Stegner's statement that the richest memories for later reminiscences usually come from a person's years stretching from age six to eleven. That assertion pushed me into thinking, "Well, that's when I was on The Ranch. I ought to think about writing about those years." But for a professor still in the classroom, a memoir would do little for his career; it might even steal him away from more immediately valuable projects. Besides, a sheep ranch boyhood might be as popular with history colleagues as last year's bird's nest.

Another encouragement to write about my sheep ranch experiences came when I was reading and reviewing Western novelist Ivan Doig's first well-known book, *This House of Sky* (1978). Doig quickly proved to me he had rich, firsthand experiences and strong memories of a sheep ranch. He knew the rhythms, routines, and rituals of the sheep camp; his book even smelled of the lambing and shearing sheds. I knew I ought to do the same with my experiences on The Ranch. Again, professorial duties and the low status of sheepherding stories turned me away. No John Wayne or Clint Eastwood had immortalized a herder as they had cowboys and gunslingers. The Ranch would have to come later.

That time came in 2018 when the Happy Valley Library near my home in Clackamas, Oregon, launched a writing group. The reference librarian, Doug Jones, with whom I had become good friends and who had helped me often with my research, asked me to head up a new writing group. I owed him one—or more—and agreed to shepherd the scribblers' outfit.

The group leader was expected to provide two to three newly written pages for the two monthly meetings. What was I to write about? The Ranch story quickly flashed into my mind. So, during the course of a year or so, I turned out the promised pages, hoping to push toward a book. Another delay shoved things off track when the group suddenly ended, meaning I now felt no pressure to turn out the monthly five pages or so on The Ranch.

In 2020, when the coronavirus pandemic hit and my wife and I were shuttered in our house, I was able to finish up all my other promised projects and return to The Ranch story. I decided to change my earlier plans; instead of only a memoir, I would now link memory and history. My story would take on more complexity and meaning if seen within the concise circumferences of eastern Washington landscapes, of my Dad's Basque backgrounds, and sheep ranching in the American West. The following pages attempt, briefly, to cord together my recollections of eastern Washington topography and major trends in Basque immigration, regional history, and sheep ranching from the 1920s into the early 1950s.

I appreciate the aid I have received from several persons in preparing this memoir. They include my brother, Dan; my sisters-in-law, Kathie and Julie; and my wife, Joyce. Also, Linda Bathgate of Washington State University Press and an anonymous manuscript reader selected by the press made helpful suggestions for revisions. Last but not least, I am indebted to several editors and publishers for their permission to use bits of my previous writing in this book. Those editors and publishers are listed in the bibliography.

I also apologize ahead of time for the uncertainty of the spelling of several names. I lack the needed sources to ascertain exact spellings.

PROLOGUE

The Etulains were on their way out to The Ranch, east of Ritzville. Several carloads of the family gradually made their way along the paved country roads bordering The Ranch. We three Etulain sons—Ken, Dan, and I—who had grown up in this isolated place, stopped our cars. We wanted to brag to the younger and mostly town- and city-bred Etulains about the heroic quality of the woven-wire and barbed-wire fences we had worked on so arduously as boys. One son-in-law, in a moment of epiphany, catching an illuminating glimpse of the possible connections between the Etulain sons and this demanding boyhood scene, quickly spoke up: "This explains a lot." Jeers and hearty chuckles broke out, and with the laughter nods of agreement.

In the next few days, I too began to ponder the meanings of the same connections. Were there holdovers and shaping links between my earliest days and later years? Had my sheep ranch experiences in this lonely setting, with Mom and Dad and my two brothers, put their marks on me? I pondered that possibility.

The eightieth birthday of my mother, Mary Etulain, in 1994 was the reason for the Etulain family reunion. On the way to see Mom in Moses Lake, we decided to visit the four places where we had grown up and to travel through other areas we remembered. The trip would begin in St. Maries, Idaho, where the Etulains spent summers. From there, we would drive down through the Palouse Country and over to The Ranch in eastern Adams County. Then on to a short visit in Ellensburg and back to Moses Lake.

Even before I planned out our itinerary in 1994, I wondered what I would remember and think when revisiting these boyhood sites.

Since memories are often uneasy marriages of facts and mythic notions blowing in the wind, I fretted about what I would experience during the reunion jaunt. Would I recall more and see the long-range ties from those earliest times to where I was now?

Most of all, I thought about The Ranch, that distant, sprawling sheep ranch twenty miles outside Ritzville. That's where the Etulain family had come together, where Dad and Mom first lived after their marriage in 1936 and where we three Etulain boys grew up. My memories of those experiences were warm and expansive, but would they prove to be so when we returned to our boyhood sheep country and looked at those experiences through middle-aged eyes?

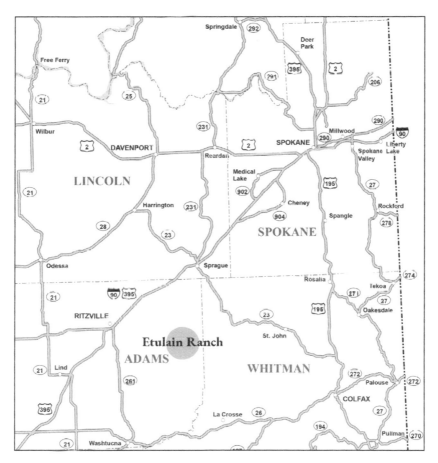

The Etulain ranch was located on Harder Road, 25 miles southeast of Ritzville at the eastern end of Adams County and about 60 to 70 miles southwest of Spokane. It is now known as Figure 50 Ranch.

1

THE LAY OF THE LAND AND THE RANCH LAYOUT

T he Etulain sheep ranch lay among rock ridges, carved-out coulees, rounded hills, and scattered grasslands in eastern Washington, twenty miles east of the town of Ritzville and nearly seventy miles south of Spokane. It was located close to the eastern edge of the Columbia Plateau, about forty to fifty miles west of the rich, wheat-farming areas of the Palouse Country. Sprawling over nearly 10,000 deeded and rented acres, our ranch included a run of landforms typical of the immediate area: rich bunchgrass flatlands, scattered small lakes, domed hills, small valleys, and rocks—our best crop, we loved to tell others, was rocks. We were in the Channeled Scablands of the Columbia Plateau.

Our ranchlands had an ancient history. Over the centuries, original nomadic peoples, first visitors, and the earliest white resettlers attempted to explain the topography of the scablands. Indigenous peoples provided the earliest stories to explain the unusual landscapes they encountered in crossing the Columbia Plateau, which stretched about 250 miles north to south and 200 miles east to west. These relatively flat, dry, and treeless areas did not beckon most early humans to the area.

Much later, geologists use origin stories to explain the land surfaces of the plateau. Not all geologists agree (surprise) and, like historians, have a variety of versions about the scablands development. But most think that huge ice dams formed in northwestern Montana on the Clark Fork River, broke open, flooded south near Spokane, rushed southward to the Snake and Columbia rivers and down those river canyons, and exited out eventually into the Pacific Ocean. The first of the large dams may have formed more than a million years ago and others as recently as 12,000 to 15,000 years in the past.

Some geologists think one of the more recent Missoula floods did the most to produce the Channeled Scablands. They suspect the ice dam backed up as much water as Lake Erie and Lake Ontario now contain and may have surged more than fifty miles an hour down to the Snake and Columbia. The wall of water, containing debris and ice, roared through eastern Washington, washed away a strip of the region's top layers, and carried that rich soil down the Columbia, down the Willamette Valley near Portland as far south as Eugene, before emptying into the Pacific. The historic flood was powerful enough to even scar the basalt rocks and carry "erratics" (giant boulders) into Oregon.

The Missoula floods cut a swath through eastern Washington, stretching from the Columbia River on the west to the Palouse Country on the east. Later, when subsequent visitors traveled across what is now the state of Washington, they often mentioned how the land surfaces dramatically changed after they crossed the Palouse and how the terrain shifted once again after they arrived in the Kittitas Valley west of the Columbia.

Over the years, numerous visitors scouted the plateau with varying reactions. From the mid-nineteenth century onward, conflicts with Indians and mining booms brought newcomers who crisscrossed parts of the Columbia Plateau. The ongoing clashes with Indians brought in military groups; mining discoveries to the east of the plateau (in Idaho) drew miners; and Washington's establishment as a territory in 1853 beckoned new immigrants.

None of these happenings had a major, lasting shaping force on the more central portions of the plateau. Other events also glancingly impacted the development of interior eastern Washington. The Oregon Trail brought settlers and livestock in the 1840s and into the 1860s, but their presence mainly impacted Oregon's Willamette Valley. Another consequence of a different type in the 1860s was Mullan Road, a military route connecting Fort Benton on the Missouri River in western Montana with Fort Walla Walla, and perhaps the Snake River. Less than a century later Mullan Road had become an intriguing but ancient relic on the eastern end of the Etulain sheep ranch.

In the 1860s, sheepmen first established flocks in the Yakima and Walla Walla areas where abundant grasses and water were readily available. As the mining booms tapered off, sheepmen were less likely to drive their flocks inland to deliver to hungry miners. The sheepmen more often resided on the edges of the plateau area—northeastern Oregon, Walla Walla, and Yakima; they had not yet entered the central Columbia Basin areas. As cultural geographer D. W. Meinig puts it, in the early 1870s, the "northern country between the scablands and the curving Columbia lay virtually untouched."

The 1880s were an expansive period for the interior Pacific Northwest, and that booming era continued a decade or two into the twentieth century. Cattle ranching expanded. The arrival of railroads, especially the Northern Pacific and its gradually expanding network of branch lines, opened the scablands in a way that no previous development had. Now two-way transportation was available: needed resources were shipped into the isolated areas of eastern Washington and the means for sheepmen to ship out their lambs and wool were available. The blizzard of publicity, in the form of railroad-produced come-on pamphlets trumpeting rich possibilities for farmers and

livestockmen, were emotion-enhancing invitations for hundreds—
and even thousands—of land-hungry newcomers.

After the Northern Pacific arrived at the Pacific Coast, in a round-
about manner in 1883, other lines followed. James J. Hill's privately
financed Great Northern, for example, crossed the far-northern parts
of the West, from St. Paul, Minnesota, to Seattle. It was completed
in 1893. Sixteen years later the Milwaukee Road finished its expansion from the Midwest to the Puget Sound area, with a route directly
through Adams County and the Channeled Scablands. At much
the same time, the Spokane, Portland and Seattle Railway (SP&S),
hatched by the Great Northern and Northern Pacific, built south from
Spokane, along the northern shore of the Columbia toward Portland,
and north to Seattle. This expanding railroad network was invaluable
to eastern Washington sheepmen. Now they had much quicker ways
to ship in needed hay and grain and ship out marketable lambs and
tons of wool.

Not surprisingly, enterprising sheepmen began to establish sizable
ranches in various segments of the plateau area. In the 1880s, the
McGregor brothers and their families came to the Hooper region in
Whitman County. Over the coming decades the McGregors became
leading entrepreneurs in land, livestock, and fertilizer. In the same
decade, the Harder family arrived near Kahlotus, Franklin County,
and through their sons and daughters became one of the largest landowners in the state of Washington. Over the years, they were sheep,
cattle, and grain raisers. In the 1890s, the Coffin brothers (especially H.
Stanley Coffin II) established themselves in the Yakima area, both to
the north toward Ellensburg, and south down the Yakima Valley. Later,
about 1910, Tom Drumheller, former football quarterback and lawyer,
purchased lands near Ephrata and became one of the state's leading
sheep ranchers. He was also a long-time leader in the Washington Wool
Growers Association. Ellis Ragan, Alec Dunnett, Archie Prior, David
Longmire, and the Martinez family—all from the Yakima area or the
Yakima Valley—established themselves as important sheepmen in the

early twentieth century.

These expanding sheep ranchers—in size, number, and importance—opened the door for much-needed sheepherders. Since Americans had never placed a high priority on sheepherding versus cowboying, herders tended to come from elsewhere. Some immigrated from Scotland or Ireland, but increasingly those in eastern Washington came from the Basque country in the Pyrenees Mountains on the border between Spain and France. Among these incoming Basque herders was my father, Sebastian Etulain. He arrived in Yakima on 11 May 1921.

As we shall see in the next chapter, in the early 1920s my father served as a herder in the Yakima Valley for a few years. Then, later in the decade, he encountered for the first time the eastern Washington scablands as a herder for a Yakima sheepman. He fell in love with the ranch country he encountered and later tried to visit his enthusiasm for the area on Mom and her three boys. Mom signed on, but the sons were reluctant to join Dad's daylight-to-dark work schedules. They were more taken with sports, girls, and, especially, pranks.

Increasingly, in the late 1920s and early 1930s, Dad dreamed of advancing from herder to sheepman and ranch owner. In 1929, Dad left his herding, joined his older brother Juan in a sheep partnership, and rented the McCall Ranch in eastern Adams County. The Etulain brothers continued to enlarge their bands of sheep before deciding to move in new directions. In 1936, they dissolved the partnership by dividing their sheep, and Juan moved to Sunnyside, Washington, where he bought a large, 15,000-acre ranch in the Rattlesnake Hills. In the same year, Dad bought the McCall Ranch and married my mother, Mary Gillard Foster.

The Etulain ranch lay within the eastern Washington scablands. The ranch landscapes were a combination of rangelands and scab rocks jutting in the background.

The size and location of The Ranch were matters of controversy when the Etulains tried to describe their ranch layout. Fellow students in Ritzville, scions of German and Russian farm families, could not understand—or believe—our stories about a spreading ranch of 10,000 acres (8,800 deeded and 1,200 rented). Their wheat farms were usually a section (640 acres) in size but rarely more than two sections (1,280 acres). Nor did they understand much about bringing in loads of hay and grain (oats, barley, pea pellets) to feed sheep, which sometimes ran to 7,000–8,000 ewes and their lambs. And after World War II, ranch operations expanded to include up to 1,000 cattle.

The location of The Ranch brought on challenges. We lived far from town on semifinished roads, which brought enormous challenges throughout the year. Travel during snowy and icy winter days could be hazardous, but the summer was difficult too, especially when we found ourselves dodging behemoth, overloaded wheat trucks during that season's harvest. The distance also impacted our schooling. Our one-room schoolhouse sat about ten miles from our ranch house, without any buses available for our transportation. We gradually realized how isolated we were from everything.

Even before I was born in 1938, Dad was laying out an expansive home place from which to direct his sprawling livestock ranch. Separation and need required action, with Dad moving ahead continuously in dealing with these demands as The Ranch expanded.

Separated by more than twenty miles from his nearest suppliers, Dad stocked The Ranch with feed for the burgeoning number of sheep and cattle he was amassing and the supplies they necessitated for ranch workers. Most of the merchants were situated to the east and north. Storage areas, feeding spots, eating places, and living areas came into existence, and grew apace.

About one-third of the year, abundant pasture grasses were greening-up on the ranchlands and provided sufficient fodder for the animals, especially when topped off with small amounts of grain. Another third of the year, most of the animals were in the mountains, feasting on rich mountain grasses. But during the other third of the year—the months stretching from November to March—the sheep and cattle needed purchased feed, plenty of it. Dad fed the livestock baled hay trucked or railed in from the Palouse country. Our beloved trucker, Ovie Scott, brought in hay, grain, and pea pellets from Colfax and nearby areas. The same locations provided large sacks of oats, the grain that nearly all the animals relished. This feed evidenced our important ranch links to the east—in the Palouse country and beyond.

The large amount of hay and grain needed storage areas. Dad threw up two huge hay barns, usually overflowing with baled hay. At the home place, the hay was usually chopped and fed in the corrals, but in the pastures, the bales were broken and scattered in feeding sites. The oats and other grains were stored in an old, rat-infested concrete granary that probably predated Dad's time. Dad divided the sacks of

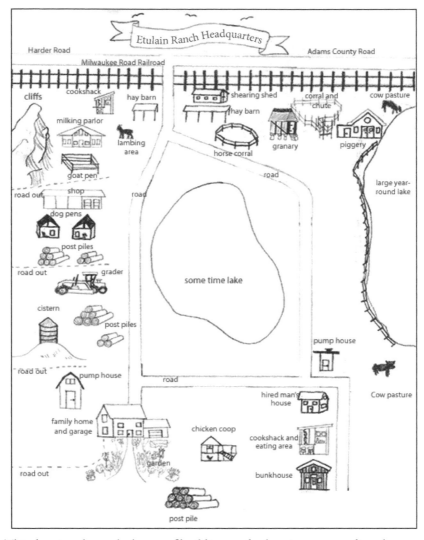

This drawing shows the layout of buildings and other sites surrounding the home site at the Etulain sheep ranch. Map drawn by Shana Huang, based on author's draft.

grain into half-sacks of fifty pounds each and poured the contents into scattered troughs at the home place or in other sites spread around The Ranch.

Scattered around the home site circle were several other essential buildings. The corrals and catch pens served for lambing and calving times and for preparing livestock for sale. The piggery, next to our sprawling lake, provided a stinky home for several hogs.

Water supply on The Ranch was particularly important, so a complex water system was laid out around the home place circle. A pump house to the west of our home sent the water up high to a cistern even farther west, perched on a nearby hill. From that height, pressure downward sent water supplies flowing to several watering tanks in the corrals and to our living areas.

Water supplies for our sheep and cattle also created large challenges on the spreading ranch. To meet that challenge, Dad organized at least a half dozen and sometimes up to ten watering spots. At those places were wells, pumps, tanks, and water troughs. One of the major duties for herders and hired men was to check these watering spots, nearly daily, to make sure our ranch animals got all the needed water. At some of these places there was a small cabin or camp wagon in which the herders lived and looked after the sheep and cattle. These sites and the home place were connected to a series of roads, although sometimes the roads were little more than two tire tracks in the dirt. None were paved.

Other vital segments of The Ranch headquarters circled around in front of our house. To the north and west were the milking parlor and creamery and, next to them, the goat pen to keep those stubborn four-footed rascals separate from the sheep. Moving south was the blacksmith shop, where a forge, vises, and several other tools helped us to shoe our horses and repair ranch tools and implements.

The dog pens were especially full during the winter months because it was dangerous to allow wild-tempered dogs to run loose without disciplined work to do. If left too much alone, they would get into trouble by chasing sheep and one another in unsupervised doggie gangs. In the spring when we unpenned our twenty or more dogs, there was usually a violent—if not deadly—dog fight as the canines who thought they were the leaders fought to keep at the head of the pack. Once out, the dogs were divided, with as many as a half dozen tending to each band of 1,000–2,000 ewes, plus lambs.

Even farther south were the post piles. Often in the spring the fence posts were creosoted to keep them from rotting too quickly when buried later. The treated posts were central to the extensive fence-building on The Ranch. Dad seemed convinced that building fences was the best way to keep his three sons busy and out of trouble—and to turn them into men.

At the southern end of The Ranch headquarters were the houses. Our family home was a sturdy, cement-based ranch home of four bedrooms, a modern kitchen, a family room, and an expansive living room. And Dad's office—filled with records and papers and, most important for us always-on-the-hunt sons, a reservoir cache of hard candy. We boys retreated there for handouts before bed each night. Sometimes we even sneaked in to steal sweets when the folks were away on a trip. Dad got wise to our thievery, however, because in getting into his locked office, we had to climb into the attic in the other end of the house, crawl over the attic cross timbers, descend through a removable attic cover into Dad's office, and grab our stolen sweets. Dad discovered our robbery because we had scattered (unnoticed) attic insulation on his office floor. There was also a full basement, including a laundry area, shelves of canned fruit, and numerous stacks of ranch supplies.

Off to the east were three other buildings. The hired man's house, although sturdy, was hardscrabble: inexpensively built and unattractive. Next, to the south, was the cook shack and dining area, where our ranch cook, Mrs. Allegria, prepared large, substantial meals for the herders and for larger numbers of other men during lambing and shearing times. After the cook shack was the bunkhouse with beds for up to about ten men with a privy out back.

At first, The Ranch had no electricity, telephone, or indoor bathroom. Pres. Franklin D. Roosevelt's New Deal programs helped to remedy these needs. The Rural Electrification Administration (REA) brought electricity to farms and ranches in the early 1940s. Before the REA came, Dad had a gasoline-fired generator that produced enough electricity for minimal uses. But the lights had to go out early because

Dad, who went to bed early, turned off the generator every night. A telephone came about the same time, a party line. Then we had to deal with what we thought was an eavesdropping neighbor lady who gossiped all our overheard family news. We remember, too, when no more trips to the outhouse behind the garage were needed. A new bathroom was built, one right next to brother Dan's and my bedroom. Of course, we then had to have Saturday night baths in the new bathtub—whether we needed them or not.

One of the untoward events that sometimes dragged us away, reluctantly but necessarily, from the home place was to fight fires. Grass fires were one of the largest dangers Dad had to face on The Ranch. Sometimes they were ignited by cigarettes carelessly thrown from a passing car or, though much less likely, by a lightning strike and especially sparks from coal-fired locomotives. Whatever the cause, the fires were frightening and destructive. And, because of distance and isolation, the fires might burn for several hours before they were discovered.

Once Dad was made aware of a fire on The Ranch, he roared into high gear. He loaded a multi-gallon tank on the back of his Chevy truck. He also placed backpack fire extinguishers in the pickup and called all available hands (including the Etulain boys) to become instant fire fighters. Just before we headed away from the home place, he'd try to contact the Ritzville Fire Department to let them know about the fire—even before he knew much about the extent or danger of it. We quickly drove to the fire area, with Dad driving the tank-loaded truck as close to the fire as he could. Then he would unleash the pressurized nozzles at the back of the truck tank on the fire. The rest of us helped out by moving into the fire lane with our firefighting backpacks, immediately pumping water onto as much of the fire as we could. When we ran out of water, Dad refilled our backpacks at the truck and sent us back to the sweaty and sometimes dangerous work. We hoped, all the while, the Ritzville fire truck and county firefighters would soon appear and help us. Most of the time they did. Usually, we were able to put out the fires, but often not before the fires had burned large sections of valuable pasture grasses.

For a pre-teen ranch boy, this expansive ranch layout and the varied experiences it engendered brought about memories, huge and magnificent—a magic place never to be forgotten. Growing up on a sheep ranch imparted, it seemed, pure pleasure and never-ending special blessings. But demanding work too.

2

A FARAWAY BASQUE DAD AND A SAINTLY MOM

People rarely forgot Dad. Not because of his looks, size, or thoughts. Instead, his actions, his achievements, captured and kept them. Dad obviously was born with a cocklebur in his diaper, an irritant that drove him early on until the drive became habit. Those watching him, including his wife and three sons, thought that he was a sturdy engine that knew no rest. A project, a deadline, an upset—he would go after it, like a courageous sheepdog heading off a threatening coyote. Dad's unceasing action and energy imprinted themselves on watchers. Few forgot what they had seen. And he was, after all, a mysterious Basque, personifying that enigmatic heritage.

In his earliest years, Dad bore the unmistakable imprint of his Basque heritage. As he grew older, he became less and less a Basque in social and cultural affairs. Still, to his last days he thought of himself as Basque.

Dad was born in 1902 in Eugui (or Eugi), a small mountain town in the Spanish province of Navarra, about forty miles north of the provincial capital of Pamplona. His father, Miguel Mari Etulain, was

Dad's birthplace home in Eugui, Spain.

a stonemason and a charcoal maker. Eventually his mother, Micaela Azparren (or Asparren) Etulain, bore five children: Pedro, Juan, Sebastian (my father), Juanita, and Carmen. The three boys came to Yakima as young men and Juanita arrived later as a single adult; Carmen remained in Spain. Dad's earliest years were spent in a solid, happy home. His father was a religious man, so the family attended mass each Sunday, and my dad even served as an altar boy in the town's Catholic church just two doors away.

But then disappointments invaded the Etulain household. Chief of these, my grandfather died when Dad was only nine. One day Miguel, overworked while making charcoal, lay down to rest, caught cold, and was gone very quickly. Having no way to support her five children, Micaela farmed out her sons to other families, where they earned small wages to support their mother and the two younger sisters. That early work led to limited education and demanding labor in the next few years. But Dad learned to stiff-arm and turn around his disappointments, doing so well with an agricultural job that a farmer, watching Dad's diligent work habits, promised him his farm if Dad would stay on, keep working, and eventually marry the farmer's daughter. But other, more fetching dreams began to surface when oldest brother, Pedro, came to the United States in 1917 and became a sheepherder. Two years later, in 1919, middle brother, Juan, also migrated to the Pacific Northwest to work with sheep. Both encouraged their younger brother and my father, Sebastian, to join them in central Washington. If these were pulls to the United States, a push also helped move Dad out of Spain. The country was embroiled in a war involving battles in North Africa, and many Basque young men were battlefield casualties. Mother Micaela encouraged her sons to go west to America to avoid the dangerous war.

So, in 1921, shortly before his nineteenth birthday, my father embarked on his epic trip to the United States. The first leg was by boat across the Atlantic, the next had him traversing by rail across the country—all the way to the Far Northwest, arriving at Wallula, Washington, and then to Yakima on May 11. On the trip, he did as many Basque young men had done. Off the boat in New York City, he checked into Valentín Aguirre's Basque boardinghouse and got helpful directions for his trip across the country. Dad always remembered the difficulty he had in obtaining food on the train trip because he lacked the English words to express what he wanted to eat. A further problem came in a misread sign: Dad had a sign around his neck for Wallula, Washington, a reminder that at that junction he would catch another train for Yakima. But the train official saw the sign as Walla Walla. So, in addition to all the other challenges, Dad was delivered to the wrong place and had to figure out how to get, finally, to Yakima.

Dad faced several large challenges once he arrived in Yakima. He had borrowed $250 from Juan, now herding sheep near Yakima. Dad spoke Basque and Spanish, had minimal schooling (in Spanish), no sure job, and had never been more than fifteen miles away from his hometown of Eugui. With a bleak future in the Basque Country pushing him out, and an American dream beckoning, Dad arrived hoping to find success. His willingness to take risks like this defined his entire life.

A few days after his arrival, Dad was already herding a band of sheep in the Yakima Valley, away from others, alone with the woolies. He had had no previous experience with sheep, only cattle. Later, he recalled how difficult those first weeks were; he was "sheeped," or depressed, lonesome, and shaken within the shadows of unfamiliarity and isolation—without money, English fluency, and contacts, alone among the sheep. He even admitted to crying in those first depressing days.

In the next weeks and months, stretching over a handful of years, Dad exhibited his tenacity and ambition as he learned the demands of open-range sheep ranching in the American West. Sheep ranchers hired herders and sent them out in jerry-built camp or sheep wagons to tend bands of 1,000–2,000 sheep. Most of the herding from fall to spring—and through the tough winter months—occurred near the home place. But in the summers, the herders and their bands headed into the high country—near at hand or no more than 200–300 miles distant, where summer pastures with fresh green grazing areas summoned the ranchers. Warm to hot summers dried up grasses on home places and forced ranchers to buy hay and keep their bands at home, or, less expensively, trail or ship their ewes and marketable lambs to the higher, more verdant mountain meadows. Because bears, wolves, and coyotes were even more threatening in the mountains, and timber and brush created additional challenges, a second ranch worker—a camptender—joined herders in the mountains.

A pack of ragtag, enthusiastic dogs, sometimes as many as five or six, were protectors of the bands and companions for the men. While herders kept the bands moving into new mountain pastures, camptenders transferred camp wagons and other equipment to the new locations. Usually, owners or ranch foremen made weekly trips to the mountains to deliver new food supplies, take care of band needs, and check in on herders and camptenders. Most of the time Dad was a herder; his cooking talents were almost nonexistent. Within a half-dozen years, Dad had learned the mysterious sheepherding system and, true to his ambitious character, looked ahead for something better.

As was true for many young Basque sheepherders, family connections played a central role for Dad in the next few years. He went to work first for his uncle Martin Etulain, who had been living in the Yakima area for a few years. With penny-pinching tightness and a never-stop work ethic, Uncle Martin had moved from herder to owning small bands of ewes. Now he was in partnership with Yakima sheepman Ellis Ragan, for whom Dad worked later. Even before Uncle Martin came to Yakima, other family members from Eugui had been working in the Pacific Northwest herding sheep. That meant that Dad was continuing a family tradition underway nearly twenty years when he came to the American West.

There was a further challenge: Uncle Martin was not easy to work for. As Dad put it, "the dogs were good company, but Uncle Martin was not." After herding Uncle Martin's sheep in the mountains between Yakima and Ellensburg, Dad transferred to work for other sheepmen when Uncle Martin sold some of his ewes. Ellis Ragan, Alec Dunnett, and David Longmire were Yakima sheep ranchers Dad worked for in the early 1920s. These men paid herders $65 to $85 per month.

Wanting to become a US citizen, Dad decided he needed more knowledge of American history and government. So, one winter he attended a seventh-grade American history class in the Yakima area to gain the needed information. He liked to tell us that his experiences in the class were doubly encouraging because some of the young girls flirted with the handsome, older guy. But the schooling worked; Dad became a citizen.

In 1927, Dad returned to herd sheep for Uncle Martin, in part because his uncle was willing to pay wages in ewes. For two years, Dad continued that work, but decided that he and his brother Juan would strike out on their own as sheepmen. Uncle Martin was unhappy about that proposal but agreed to give Dad 800 ewes for back pay in September 1929. Dad purchased another 400 ewes, and together he and Juan rented some of the McCall range east of Ritzville (which later became the Etulain ranch). One month later the disastrous Depression hit, with the newly purchased ewes at $14 per head plummeting in value. By the next year, prices dropped even further, with lambs bringing only three cents a pound even after a costly trip east. Fortunately, the Woolgrowers Finance Company supported the Etulain brothers through the near-disastrous two years. By 1931, prices turned around, expenses lowered, and the brothers were able to pay their debts and make a few dollars. They even began renting land near St. Maries, Idaho, for summer grazing.

Things changed dramatically in 1932. Uncle Martin died when, falling asleep, his car slid off into the Yakima River, and he drowned. Martin's brother Fermín was set to inherit the considerable estate of $150,000–$200,000. But just before his untimely death, Uncle Martin had taken steps to make Dad his heir. Knowing Martin's intentions, his lawyer appraised Martin's ewes as worth only $1 per head and allowed Dad to purchase the uncle's sheep at that astoundingly low price. This extraordinary turn of events allowed Dad and Uncle Juan to double the size of their bands by the end of 1932. Now, they needed more space for their suddenly expanded flocks.

Robert McCall, the owner of the McCall lands that Dad, Uncle Juan, and Uncle Martin had rented, was unable to keep up on his land payments because of the Depression. The bank assumed control of the McCall Ranch and sold its ewes for $4 a head to the Etulain brothers. The next year those ewes brought $8 a head in Chicago. The bank holding the note on the McCall land offered to sell it to Dad on a 15-year plan. Beginning in 1936, he paid off The Ranch in four years.

Meanwhile, two important happenings changed the direction of Dad's life. About 1936, he and Uncle Juan decided it was time to establish two different ranches rather than to remain in a partnership. Leaving the McCall Ranch, Uncle Juan took his share of the sheep and moved to Sunnyside, Washington, where he purchased a 15,000-acre ranch located nine miles outside town.

The other life-changing event for Dad: at age thirty-three, he found a wife. Mary Gillard Foster, the mother of a young son and a divorcée, was cooking at a nearby Harder family sheep camp during lambing time. As Dad told me later, they met one another and after "tasting her cooking [Dad] fell in love with her." They married in 1936. Soon two sons were born to Sebastian and Mary: my brother Dan (1937) and I (1938). By the end of the 1930s everything had greatly changed for Dad: he was a husband, a father to three sons (he had adopted Mary's son Kenneth), and an owner of a large sheep ranch with nearly 7,000 ewes and lambs.

During the 1930s, Dad clearly exhibited the character traits that his friends and family would long recall. He was embracing the dream that if he worked hard he could overcome his lack of formal education, limited occupational skills, financial insecurities, and sense of the innocence of American culture. Hard work became Dad's doctrine of life, which he resolutely exhibited and attempted to pass on to his fellow laborers and, later, to his three reluctant sons.

The family canonized Mom as a peacemaker and encourager. Although her grassroots background ill-prepared her for life with a driven, immigrant husband and three recalcitrant sons, Mom's patience and people skills won out. New, challenging duties proved not to be barriers but open avenues that helped her shape her attitudes and actions. By her mid-20s, her life had moved in three very different directions. First, the traditional: Mom's parents were of the sod house variety. Beginning in southern Minnesota, they came west—first to the Dakotas and then, before 1900, to the new state of Washington. Her father remained a lifetime man of the soil, a farmer who never owned land, always renting. Her mother, a sturdy, dependable housewife, had raised five children to adulthood, but lost two others in infancy. Mom—Mary Lou Gillard—was born in 1914 in Wapato, Washington, and grew up in that central Washington farm and ranch country. She was the youngest in the family by fifteen years. Her brothers and sisters were all away from home when she grew up with her mother and father.

Nearly everything in Mom's life during her first eighteen years was traditional—even commonplace. Her father and mother, aged 52 and 38 respectively when she was born, were stable, at-home parents. They were diligent, religious, and affable. Mom's first years were as a lone girl growing up with her parents.

Mom's mom, Jennie Wiley Gillard, was a key family figure—for our mother as well as for The Ranch grandsons. Grandma Gillard had a warm heart, one that opened her to helping her family and neighbors. For example, when Uncle Juan ran sheep near the Gillard farm close to Wapato, Washington, she helped him with his English, pointed to needed water sources for his sheep, and even tried to learn Spanish from him. Homespun, if not a bit unkempt, Grandma visited us often, especially after she became a widow. (We Etulain boys never met Grandpa Gillard.) I remembered how much she loved Mom, calling her "Maidy," and the kindness she showered on us boys.

But there was no question that Mom was raised in a sheltered home with aging parents. Born in the United States, she nevertheless more than likely qualified as an "innocent abroad." That sheltered life of innocence probably led to a second stage in her life, which veered off in a dramatic, unexpected direction. The traditional and commonplace flew out the window on 30 September 1932, when, at age eighteen and between her junior and senior years of high school, Mom married Luther Foster, a 39-year-old widower with several children, some of whom were nearly as old as she. Foster seemed in a hurry to replace his first wife who, it was rumored, had died while trying to carry out a self-induced abortion. Mystery surrounds the quick marriage; Mom refused, at first, to talk about her marriage to Foster. She stayed out of her senior year of high school, had son Kenneth Duane on June 24, 1933, and then returned for her last year of schooling. The brief marriage soon crumbled, and divorce quickly followed. Still in her teens, Mom was already a divorcée with a young child.

Disappointed and crestfallen about what had occurred, Mom kept secret her early marriage and the identity of Kenny's father. Her sons did not know until they were ten years and older that Mom had had an earlier marriage and that Kenny was a half-brother to younger sons Danny and Dicky. The news came suddenly. One day when Dan and I were about nine or ten, cousin Don Knight was visiting and fired a dramatic informational question at us: "Do you guys know that Ken is not your real brother, he is your half-brother?" Upset, we dashed home and told Mom what Don had said, asked if that was true, and questioned why she hadn't told us about Ken's heritage. She dodged a pointed interrogative bullet by saying, offhandedly, "Well I didn't think you guys would be interested in that." Even after the bare details were known, no one, probably sensing Mom's wishes, ever talked much about the verboten subject. Marriages, births, and similar celebrations were never specifically dated. Church membership was also impossible because the Church of the Nazarene, at that time, did not allow divorcées to become members. Mom's early, unsuccessful marriage remained a family secret never fully revealed or measured.

The next notable change in Mom's life occurred when she married Dad in 1936. The new loads it created were novel—and heavy. Not only was she taking on a new husband and keeping up with her young son, two younger sons soon joined the new family. Dad brought financial support and stability that she had not known in her first marriage, but his needs were much more than anything Mom had previously experienced. How Mom struggled through those first years is not clear. She never shared those burdens, and her sons seemed unaware of what she had had to bear.

A few glimpses of those early hard times were revealed later because some of the struggles continued into our times of recognition. Dad was so demanding, so bent on success, so pushed to move beyond others, he had little time to be a husband and father. We sons sometimes wondered, later, if Mom, so heavily burdened with daily duties and so pushed by Dad's demands, might have thought of leaving The Ranch.

Dad and Mom about the time of their marriage in 1936.

But what would a woman in her late twenties into her thirties, with three young sons and no training or education, do to support herself and her children? Perhaps, we thought, Mom realized she was trapped but could find victory in soldiering on and at least staying even with demands and schedules. Sainthood was beginning.

Mom exhibited her social ambitions for her family in several ways. Education topped the list. Even before we became teenagers, Mom would point out a person in town or the church and say, "Well, he has a college education" or "She is college-educated." Perhaps Mom planted these seeds because our early schooling seemed so spotty and possibly inferior, but her devotion to education may have also been motivated by the fact that she had not gained the education that she envisioned for her sons. When one considers that Ken eventually earned an engineering degree, Dan a doctorate in education, and I a doctorate in history, Mom won out in her educational ambitions for her sons.

More hazy but nonetheless evident was Mom's desire to be socially acceptable and to make sure her family achieved the same status. This desire for social acceptance may have been the major reason she chose not to speak about her early marriage and divorce. The key word was "refined." When she was attracted to a person's actions, ideas, and appearance, she frequently referred to that person as "refined." In our home, we frequently heard Mom say, "We don't do things like that" or "We don't talk like that." In another way, Mom tried to achieve refinement for her sons by making sure they had spiffy clothes, looked "dressed up," and later drove nice cars. Her dreams for Ken, Dan, and me also led to possible cultural achievements: she made sure each of us tried to play the piano and, when that did not work, she promoted later attempts at horn playing and violins. We boys, however, thought our hands fit better into baseball gloves than onto musical instruments. She enjoyed, too, shopping in the upscale stores in Spokane: the Bon Marche, the Crescent, and Nordstrom shoes. Mom was a tireless, well-oiled shopping machine. She should have worn a sign on her back, "This shopper stops quickly and often. Take care."

Mom was likewise a peacemaker, especially in her sometimes tension-filled connection with Dad. It was only natural for Dad, having begun work as a preteenager, to think his sons ought to do the same. Beginning very early, he found small chores for us on The Ranch. We could go get the milk cows for night milking; we could help fill the pig troughs; we could help sack grain in the granary; and we could carry out small duties at lambing time. When we complained about not having enough time for our delights, including sports, Mom would urge Dad to give us some time off. That eventually meant each of us could play one sport—as long as we also kept up with assigned duties like milking the cows.

One incident reveals how Mom could be a peacemaker—and literally save our hides. Someone had turned on and left running a water faucet in The Ranch corral, draining the large water cistern on the hill near our house. Dad was afire with blame—and it nearly torched us. We ran to Mom and crouched behind the piano where Mom was when Dad approached; we tearfully told Mom we had not left the water on. Mom literally held Dad off, and it was soon revealed that Johnny, a young six-year-old staying with us, was the culprit. Mom saved us from the licking that Dad had in mind for us boys.

Mom also provided links to other families. Other than Uncle Juan, we knew virtually nothing about Dad's family since so many of his extended family remained in Spain and France. Uncle Pedro had come to the United States but disappeared in southern California, where he became a waiter at an upscale restaurant. We rarely saw him. But we did connect with Mom's relatives. We frequently drove over to nearby Moses Lake, where we visited with Mom's niece Ruth Radach, her husband Ray, and their kids. Ray was a wheat farmer, and he and Dad could talk farming but not much about ranching. It was Mom's attachment to Ruth, her brother's daughter, that kept us linked to the Radachs. Even closer was our relationship with Mom's next older sister, Giralda, her farmer-husband Mac Knight, and their grown kids. Mac and Giralda Knight were as nice to the Etulain kids as anyone else in our early lives. They seemed to think of us as their kids too. A trip to Union Gap or out to their rented farm on the Yakama Reservation in the valley was an unforgettable jaunt. Mom was clearly the glue for our ties with her surrounding family.

How did Mom become a saint? Perhaps having to deal with the decidedly unsaintly men in her life. Living with a demanding, hard-headed Basco (person of Basque heritage) for half a century. Trying to raise three rascally sons. Isn't that like trying to herd coyotes? Mom learned, early on, that disappointments and failures should not be barriers and chasms but foundations on which to build a life and examples for others on how life could be lived, despite a truckload of duties on her back.

3

DICKY COMES
ON THE SCENE

was born Richard Wayne Etulain on 26 August 1938 in Wapato, Washington. In fact, all of us, save Dad—that is, Mom and her three sons—were born in Wapato. Mom gave birth to all of her boys in a "laying in" home in Wapato—so as to be near her mother for birthing help. Mom soon brought me back to The Ranch, where I joined brothers Kenny and Danny and where I'd be with them for slightly more than the next eleven years.

My first memories of ranch life are vague and distant, yet I recall gradually becoming accustomed to the daily, weekly, and yearly rhythms that governed our everyday lives even before entering school. I think I was able to discern these patterns and regularity at a later time; but as a preschooler, they seemed to just happen, and over time my brothers and I got used to them.

For the most part, Dad set up the system. Up early, around five or six in the morning to do needed daily chores, he returned to the house about seven and expected Mom to have a large breakfast ready—and she did. Usually, we all gorged ourselves on hotcakes or French toast, eggs, and bacon. Dad had his once-a-day cup of coffee, and we boys downed our large glasses of milk. Lunch usually featured soup, salad,

Dicky (in the wagon) and brother Danny in the backyard of their St. Maries, Idaho, summer home.

Danny and Dicky, nearly sailor-suited twins, and Dan and Dick many years later.

and fruit. And for our largest meal at supper we feasted on a hearty meat dish (often lamb chops or roast), potatoes, salad, fruit, and a rich dessert. Dad was a happy eater, and we boys learned the same, all of us enjoying Mom's super cooking.

After breakfast, Dan and I had a lot of free time. Ken had started our country Lantz School about the time I was born, so with Ken gone daily from the scene, Dan and I set our own agendas once Mom let us out of her sight, which was quite often. I recall several favorite activities in that period up to fall 1943, when I started school.

Dirty diggings were one favorite activity. Behind the ranch house and up a nearby draw, there were a series of diggings—perhaps the leftovers from an old well and something of an animal graveyard. Dan and I dragged our shovels along and dug new trails and mini-caves in the dirt-filled areas. In some ways, the activities were dangerous: the caves sometimes collapsed and on a few occasions a new sheep carcass was thrown into our diggings. Dad warned us away from the carcasses, but we usually just moved farther on down the draw to launch new diggings.

Another segment of the preschool rhythms depended on whether Ken was available to serve as raft captain. A large lake to the east of the house remained full year-round, and when Ken could take charge (Mom wouldn't let us go unless Ken could direct things), we pushed off on our raft and dreamed of being on a wide, wide ocean. Again, dangers lurked. We could easily have fallen in where the water was too deep or overturned the raft. Even more threatening was the dirty water itself. The pigpen bordered the lake, and pig droppings drained into the lake where we skipped merrily about. Those threats never seemed to keep us off the lake.

Daily activities also included a good deal of aimless wandering near the house and outbuildings. These meanderings included visits to the pigpen to watch the pigs and throw clods at them, tramps up to the milking parlor to see the hired man milking and separating the cream and milk in the milking parlor, and calls at the blacksmith shop to watch Dad and the hired men firing up the forge and welding things. Probably our favorite visit was to the dog pen, especially in the wintertime when all the ranch dogs were penned up. We could pet our favorites, take snacks to them, and just hang out with doggie friends.

Weekly rhythms added other activities. Paramount among these were the trips to Ritzville on Saturdays and Sundays. Even before I became a first-grader, Mom encouraged me to visit the Carnegie Library in town. Probably, she needed somebody like a babysitter for her three sons while she and Dad did their important Saturday shopping, especially at the town's Safeway store. Whatever my parents' purpose, the town library was already a hangout place before I began school. I would sit in one of the easy chairs, look at kids' books, and talk with other kids—if we closely followed the librarians' ever-present shhhs.

My earliest memories likewise include the Sunday visits to the Ritzville Church of the Nazarene. Early on, the church provided opening exercises for kids, with music, prayer, and object-lesson teachings. And very soon after they offered separate classes for boys and girls. Those Sunday School meetings were my first experiences in social gatherings beyond visits from our family or relatives.

In the evenings, Mom added to our religious training by reading Bible stories just before our bedtime. She read from a large, well-illustrated Bible storybook printed just for kids. Those were gathering times for we three boys and Mom, often nearly every night. We never had similar gatherings with Dad. He was too busy with The Ranch.

Yearly rhythms quickly became part of my early boyhood life, although I doubt that I was much aware of their regularity and system before I went to school. A sheep ranch rhythm prevailed. Beginning in the fall, we'd return from St. Maries, where Mom and Dad and we three boys spent summers during the first five years of my life—up to 1944, when I was in the second grade. In the fall, back at The Ranch, there were new feeding times for the sheep when hay, grain, and other feed were trucked in from outside The Ranch. This activity often led

Dicky (left) and Danny (right) in the backyard of the sheep home ranch.

us guys to the granary or hay barns to watch the unloading of the feed. Or, to the hay barns to play on the newly stacked hay bales.

Right after Christmas, lambing started. Even before I went to school, I helped feed the bum lambs and carry feed to the ewes. Since Dad had become a full-time ranch worker in Spain by age nine, he thought it not unusual to ask his young guys to help out with ranch chores.

Although we were not involved in shearing times in April or May, we usually were at the shearing shed about a half mile from the house. And, increasingly over the years, we intermingled with the shearers' families, enjoying any kids who came with them.

In June, we were off to St. Maries in Idaho for three months of summering.

I recall being a bit mystified with town activities, including the nearby neighbors' doings, the closeness of restaurants and church, and the adjacent river, swimming areas, and railroad tracks and hoboes. During those summer months, I often thought I was in another country.

The most important change thus far in my life came in fall 1943 when I entered the first grade. I attended Lantz School from the first through the fourth grades. At the school, no more than ten students attended at a time—only five in my last year there. But I was outside home, mingling with other kids, and reading books—all important experiences for me before I turned ten. I think my lifetime addiction to books began during my time at the Lantz School, in the books we read in classes, in the encyclopedias stored out in the front hallway, and in the books I fetched from the Ritzville library.

Gradually, Dad called on us to do more on The Ranch. We brought in the milk cows at night, helped to sack grain in the granary, fed ewes in corral catch pens, and ran errands. By the time I was ten, Dad had introduced all three of us to many rudimentary ranch tasks.

The largest break in the usual ranch rhythms, I now think, came when we ended our time at the Lantz School and began attending the

Ritzville grade school in fall 1947: high school for Ken, Central [Grade] School for Dan and me. It was a long bus ride—about an hour each way—taking us away from The Ranch into town. We were thrown into another alien teacher-and-book world with new meanings and strange people. Going to school now meant something else.

The Lantz and Ritzville school experiences were at such odds with one another that I had difficulty thinking what "school" was. The size of classes, the better-prepared teachers, the more varied courses, the diverse students, and the existence of so many pretty girls and sports—these were all in the Ritzville school. Gradually, I realized that the Lantz School years had disappeared; I was now in a new kind of school. And for the most part I enjoyed schooling at Ritzville. As usual throughout my public-school years, I was satisfied to be an average student; no one yet had lit a fire of intellectual curiosity in me.

Another change in the yearly schedule at The Ranch came at the end of World War II. At age seven, I was hearing and seeing about cowboy things rather than more about sheep and sheepherders. Because of the negative economic impact of the war, Dad had sold most of his sheep and bought cattle. That meant roundups and branding were replacing lambing, shearing, and trailing to the mountains. And no more summers in St. Maries. Plus, fewer people were on The Ranch; instead of all the herders and the extra helpers during lambing and shearing times, we were down to a hired man and an occasional additional helper at roundups and branding times.

From 1945 to 1949, I never made as much of a switch in things as Dad did. Although brother Ken relished mounting his horses, Prince or Duke, Dan and I were not much involved in the cattle-raising business. True, we continued to bring in the milk cows at night, sometimes helped chase cattle in the corral and down the branding chutes, and on a few occasions went up to Spokane to the stockyards to see cattle on sale; but for the most part we still thought of ourselves as a sheepman's kids.

In fact, continuities more than changes ruled my life. I continued to attend school in Ritzville, went to town for Saturday visits, and attended church on Sunday. There were also the ongoing visits to the Ritzville library. I found little in my weekly activities to throw me off center and into new pathways.

One change, however, did make a difference. The Church of the Nazarene began to sponsor summer week-long boys, girls, and youth camps at Deer Park, several miles north of Spokane. Attending for the first time when I was nine, and terribly homesick, I went to those camps for nearly ten years—up to and including my first college years. That connection with district Nazarenes prepared the way for my ongoing tighter connection with the church and my eventual attendance and teaching at Northwest Nazarene College (now university).

When Dad announced in the summer of 1949 that he was thinking of selling The Ranch and that we would move to a smaller farm in Ellensburg, I was worried. It would be my first move to a new home, and I remembered my discomfit when transferring from the Lantz to the Ritzville schools. My ill-at-ease feeling heighted when The Ranch sold and in October 1949 we moved to Ellensburg. But things went smoothly at the new farm and at school. In fact, Dan and I moved on with farm duties, becoming cow milkers and hay makers.

And yet even in the years to come, I never forgot those first eleven years of my life. Those were the years we were at The Ranch.

4

OLDER BROTHER KENNY AND BIG BROTHER DANNY

Older brother Kenny probably thought of Dan and me as younger, pesky brothers. Four and five years older than us, Ken undoubtedly realized we were still in an infantile world he had already escaped. The back and forth among the three of us defined a good deal of the personal side of our ranch family life.

None of us were sure how much Ken knew about his more complicated past. Had he learned about his real father at the same time we did? Did he know more than Dan or I until he was about fifteen or sixteen? For us, there was nothing different about Ken after we learned he was our half-brother. But what did he think? I don't know. Like Mom, he rarely spoke about his earliest history—even after he learned much of the detail.

My first solid memories of Ken were when I was five, just beginning school, and he was ten. Before long, he became the chief of the Ranch Raiders, and Dan and I his youthful lieutenants. We followed closely wherever big brother Ken's escapades led us. He was a quiet but mischievous guy, hardly ever disagreeing openly with Mom and Dad; but behind the scenes he went his own way.

Out of sight of our parents, Ken took charge. Sometimes his actions aimed at just getting rid of his runty little brothers, pests at his heels. Once, we were riding horses, Ken on his favorite stallion, Prince, Dan and I on the trusty mare, Toots. Tired of our tagging along, Ken slapped the rear end of the normally placid Toots and shooed her away, sending her trotting toward home. Dan and I bounced around on Toots, bareback and trying to hold on, barely staying aboard until the mare stopped in front of the granary. Mom, hearing of what Ken had done—guess who told her?—gave him another of her Ken-directed warnings.

The Ranch Raiders with Ken at the head were often adventurous vagabonds. Heavily loaded with Dad's expectations and demands, Mom gave us plenty of space. During the late spring or early fall, before we took off or returned from our summer months in St. Maries, and on Saturdays when we didn't go to Ritzville for those dreaded music lessons, we were off on bike-riding jaunts. Mom packed us a lunch and told us to be careful, to stay out of trouble, and to be back for supper. Often we headed north, across the Milwaukee Road tracks and out to the county road leading to Lamont to the east and Ritzville to the west. A favorite haunt was the agent's station on the SP&S Railway, which crossed over the Milwaukee about four or five miles from our ranch house. If the SP&S agent was gone, as he often was, into his garden Ken would lead us, and not long afterward the agent's watermelons were in ruin. And Dan and I didn't even like watermelon.

Ken also led us on homebound experiments. When Mom and Dad drove up to Spokane for a day of shopping and supplies and we were left at home, Ken dove into another of his culinary tests, all of which were verboten. All kinds of mixes and messes were tried, especially fudge, which all of us relished. Rarely did the experiments work out, so secretly down the drain they went before the folks got back from their trip.

Ken got us into trouble in one situation. He was driving the pickup back and forth to a remote lake not too far from The Ranch. He

Dicky, Danny, and Kenny standing in front of one of our "sacred" Chevrolets.

Danny, Dicky, and Kenny spiffed up to go to church in Ritzville.

decided to let Dan, then about ten or eleven, take the wheel. Soon, Dan nearly took down a fence with the side of the pickup. Of course, our story contained different details. We told Dad and Mom that another driver, at the lake, had evidently backed into the pickup while we were there. We hadn't seen him do the bad deed, so we had no further details. For once, our stretchers seemed to satisfy the folks.

Before we left The Ranch in 1949, Ken turned into a teenager. His mischievousness mounted as he discovered cars, girls, and sports—in that order. I don't recall how he talked Dad into driving the pickup to school to turn out for football, but he did. Maybe Mom talked Dad into that, as she was often our advocate for such requests. One day, I recall walking near Ritzville High School and having to jump out of the way of a careening blue Chevy pickup screeching threateningly my way. It was Ken.

Ken and his new buddy at Ritzville High School, the diminutive Stan Shell, were even more likely to break the rules when together, and were equally daring. One night Ken sneaked out with the pickup, met Shell, and they drove over to nearby Wall Lake. Mysteriously, they made it back without Mom and Dad knowing what had happened. On another day, Ken and Shell skipped school to hunt pheasants. While out in the brush, Ken heard a familiar-sounding truck, slipped behind a bush, and watched as Dad drove by on his way south. Another close encounter.

Dan and I never fell in love with ranching. Once given the opportunity later, we turned into town and city dudes, never joining the Future Farmers of America groups where we lived. Not so with Ken. He loved some things about ranching, especially horses. When Dad later thought—mistakenly for the most part—about his sons taking over the Etulain ranch holdings, it was Ken who came to mind. Even after Ken went into the military, finished college, and became an engineer, he continued loving places on the edge of town. His final residence, not far from Salt Lake City, was a small ranch with horses.

By the time we left The Ranch in 1949, Ken was a ripe teenager, loving cars, sports, and playing hooky. Those fascinations mounted, and a year or so after we had moved to a small livestock farm near Ellensburg, Ken dropped out of school, ran away from home, and soon thereafter joined the Army, where he quickly matured. Ken's adventuresome, independent spirit had led him away from our traditional, firmly anchored home. Dan and I had to find a new chief and fresh tracks to follow.

Danny and I weren't twins, but some thought so. We were fourteen months apart, but Mom dressed us alike. I got to start school a year early, because Mom saw no reason to keep Dicky at home another year. So, we were in the same class from the first grade into graduate school. Dicky and Danny must have been twins.

Our interests were different, however. Dan loved toys, trinkets, and gadgets, while I became addicted to books. Tinkertoys, marble games, and erector sets grabbed Dan's attention while I fell in with the Hardy Boys, the Chip Hilton sports stories, and even the Nancy Drew mystery series.

But sports captured both of us. Football, basketball, and especially baseball were our fascinations. Dan was a sturdy, blocky catcher, but I roamed the outfield. Neither of us, however, was very successful in getting our bats on the fast pitches and curveballs coming our way. Brother Ken and I were Yankee fans; Dan rooted for the Cleveland Indians. "Anybody but the Yankees," Dan would taunt us.

On The Ranch and in the mountains, Dan seemed less interested than I was about visiting the sheep camps. So, more often I was Dad's "sonny boy" companion, and we headed off to see the herders. I recall trying to find something to do in the mountains while Dad seemed to talk all day to them.

Because I loved books more than Dan, I suppose that helped me in some classes. I relished libraries and bookstores and ideas, while Dan veered toward the sciences and hands-on classes. Those diverging interests led, up ahead, to my becoming a history and literature teacher and Dan's embracing science teaching and then becoming a TV producer.

But that rascal Dan, more handsome than I, always seemed able to win over the "chicks" more easily and more quickly. And, doubly disgusting, he got to first base with the young ladies I wanted to attract.

Dan and I often competed, sometimes clashed. He was taller and stronger, but I was faster, scooting away from his whacking and attempted wrestling pins.

Our differences showed up in our early diverse projects. Dan created competitive games. He even put together a pinball machine that shot marbles up to the top of a board and allowed them to trickle down into slots below. He created another game via the imaginative use of backyard hoses he had placed together like an alley or chute. Down came the marbles, following the incline of the backyard, jumping over Dan-made bridges. I tried to make sure my marbles made better time than his. They rarely did.

On other occasions we worked together on chores Dad assigned to us. We were expected to bring in the milk cows for the evening milking. Sometimes that was not an easy but instead a scary task since those stubborn cows would stay in the back of the cow pasture a mile or two away from the milk house in cold and threatening weather. Sometimes we had to go out afraid, in the evening shadows. At other times, we slopped the hogs and brought in firewood. We were expected, too, to observe the butchering of cows, sheep, and hogs—to see "how things were done." The same with branding. Every so often we also fed milk to the "bum" (or orphan) lambs or spread hay into the catch pens for ewes to munch on along with their new lambs.

Dan and I shared a bedroom that had two single beds. One wall was covered with a huge map of the state of Washington, and one of our favorite games was trying to fool the other about county, county seat, and other place-names. When Dad came in to say goodnight, he would tell us to turn off the radio and the lights. Once he was gone, we took turns hiding our shortwave radio under the covers and tuning in to Sacramento baseball games on KFBK, listening to broadcaster Tony Koester and hearing about a divine Shakey's Pizza.

A few other games spiced our lives. In our final years on The Ranch, a young, newly married couple from Colville, Don and Jolene Brooks, moved down to become our hired-man family. Don loved to play basketball, so he and us Etulain boys hung a basketball hoop in the granary and shot baskets among the grain sacks—and the scampering rats and mice. On some evenings we went over to their house, about a hundred yards east of ours, to play rousing games of Monopoly or the Rook card game.

Some might have thought the Etulain brothers were as thick as thieves; maybe and maybe not. One day, Ken, Dan, and I rode our bikes down to a nearby natural declivity we called "the hole in the ground" and saw one of our camp wagons parked there, left by a herder who was out following his band. We broke into it and found some cigarettes. That was the only time in my life I smoked cigarettes. Ugh. So, maybe we were thick as thieves after all.

On a few occasions Dan would bug me. (I never bothered him, of course.) The earliest occasion I recall was him tickling my ear with a shoestring when I was trying to recite something while in school. He also was better at marbles than I, so usually my shooters and "steelies" ended up in his marble bag. That fascination with marbles got us in trouble one time. We were then in school at Ritzville, where we got into an intense marble game and missed the bus and the hour's ride home. Never again. After Mom had to make the two-hour round trip to pick us up, a paddling stick reminded us not to repeat that mistake.

On other occasions, Dan and I tried to work out something that otherwise might have gotten us in trouble. One memorable experience occurred when Mom and Dad had gone to Spokane. Dan and I got into some kind of deadly competition that involved him crawling through a very small hole in the house foundation. He started bugging me again. Teed off, I threw a rock at his face in the hole. The rock hit him square in the forehead, just above one of his eyes. (An inch or so lower and the rock might have badly damaged it.) The rock left an obvious mark on Dan's forehead, and we knew the folks would want to know what had happened. Working out a compromise, we agreed we would tell them that Dan had stumbled and banged his head on the ground. Not a good alibi, but our stealth helped us get away with it—at least on this occasion.

Through the years, Dan and I sparred a lot about ideas too, each of us thinking the other was "dead wrong" and needed to heed a better truth. Yet even with the competitions, harsh words, and flameouts, there was linkage. He was my big brother—and that was enough.

5

OFF TO SCHOOL

There it was, a wider world perched just off the edge of our sprawling ranch. Each morning during the school year, our hired man, Boyd Crider, loaded his son, Jimmy, and the three Etulain boys—Kenny, Danny, and Dicky—into the back, cab-over section of his pickup and headed off to school. It was a cold, bumpy ride through our muddy, ungraveled ranch roads.

We were off to Lantz School District 80 (in existence from 1903–47). The school was located at the corner of Benge Highway and Calloway Road, at least five miles from our home, ten miles from the nearest gas station, and even farther from a real town. The shingled, very small schoolhouse bulged with about ten desks, its entry hallway rich with books, its teacherage hooked to the back of the schoolroom. That was our school, at the rear of an outback.

But school—the teachers, classes, and books—initiated us into larger, eye-opening worlds. There were the fascinations with Abraham Lincoln and Robert E. Lee and Mark Twain's stories. Even more memorable was the elementary textbook, *Singing Wheels*, which introduced me to the pioneer West—not far removed in time from our isolated sheep ranch. And out in the entry hall were those encyclopedias, full of pictures of places and people that seemed to come from another planet, offering vicarious travel.

Students and teacher Grace Smick at Lantz School, second grade 1944–45.
Dicky and Danny are at each end of the first row; Kenny is fifth from left in back
row, next to Mrs. Smick.

Our teachers were women, and there was a new one nearly every
year. Each realized what rascals we were. They tried to teach us how
to be more gentlemanly to Georgia Ann Calloway, the only girl at the
school early on, who had to tolerate four male student barbarians.

At the Lantz School we learned other than bookish things. Of first
importance, the school introduced us to girls, since most of the time
there were no girls on our ranch. Georgia Ann was there with us all
four years, from 1943 to 1947, but we were especially taken with the
two girls that Mrs. Smick brought with her to the school when she
taught the second and third grades. Ginger was older than we were
and more attractive to Ken, but Andreana was pretty and perky and
closer to our ages. She showed us why girls might fascinate boys. We
also played pickup softball when there were enough kids for a game.
We even tried to put together a team, including the teacher and her
spouse, when we went over to the Harder School for a visit. Our rules
and play in these games came out of nowhere.

Mom kept the report cards for my four years at Lantz School:

Dicky's report card for the second grade (1944–45) at Lantz School.

Grade	Teacher	Class Grades	Teacher Comments
First	Bernice Egbert	A(1), B(7), C(2)	
Second	Grace Smick	A(6), B(3), C(1)	Needs improvements in industry
Third	Grace Smick	A(5), B(6), C(1)	
Fourth	Fay Orr	A(8), B(0), C(0)	[Mrs. Orr, I think, was anxious to retire; I was not a straight-A student]

For four years, Dan and I attended this remote Valhalla of learning. We were finding out that teachers and books were doorways to a distant, strange world. Then the Edenic school days ended when brother Kenny finished the eighth grade. Only four students remained at Lantz. The school had to close. All of us had to go elsewhere.

Our next schools were in Ritzville. The first shock was the larger size of the classes. At Lantz, there were only five students among the eight grades. Now, at Ritzville, Dan and I were among thirty to thirty-five kids in the fifth and sixth grades. The expansion gave me the feeling that the whole world had been crammed into our schoolroom.

But at Ritzville Central Grade School there were sports and girls. At noontime we played keep-away football, and I soon learned how good a classmate like Danny Schwisow would become in football when he made it into high school. But in the fifth and sixth grades, I tried to tackle him whenever I could. It didn't happen much. Tommy German was also a strong athlete, and Gary Danekas and Alan Bentz were already class leaders.

I also remember the pretty girls I was smitten with. They included Janet Ohland, Loretta Arlt, and Beverly Hennings. I should have been forewarned: brother Dan was already attracting more girlish attention than I could.

My teachers for these two grades were diligent and strong and pushed me to do better:

Grade	Teacher	Class Grades	Teacher Comments
Fifth	Irma Heily	A(1), B(3), C(2), S (2)	Needs improvement in courtesy, kindness
			Needs improvement in neat, orderly work
			Needs improvement in control of temper
			Needs improvement in writing plainly and spelling correctly
Sixth	Ovella A. Bosma	A(3), B(4), C (0), S(3)	Everything satisfactory

I remember how much I was taken with geography and history. One map of the Gran Chaco in northern Argentina sticks in my mind. We often drew—mainly traced—maps, colored them, and then inked in the names of places. I think studying geography and history was cathartic. The Etulain family didn't travel much, following Dad's determination to stay at home and address demanding duties, so looking at maps and examining and dreaming about the history of exotic, faraway places like Dad's Basque country, the eastern United States, and even Seattle and Spokane were vicarious experiences, replacing and standing in for actual trips as a tourist or sightseer.

Another memory from our fifth- and sixth-grade classroom years remains strong. Class enrollments bulged at the main Ritzville Central School building located near the center of town, so our class was farmed out to the back rooms of the high school. But the memorable part was that we were right next to the home economics classroom. All day the wonderful aromas of the meals the young students (all

Dicky and Danny in the sixth grade at Ritzville Central School, 1948–49; Ovella A. Bosma, teacher. Dicky, third from the right in the first row; Danny, fourth from the right in the second row.

girls then) were preparing wafted into our classroom. It was a daily distraction for always-hungry fifth- and sixth-graders.

Mom was tireless in spiffing us up for school. Not only did she dress us in new clothes from the JC Penney Company and Ritzville Trading Company stores, but also pants and shirts gathered from quick trips to Spokane stores. And our hair. Mom believed boys needed to have hair that remained arranged and attractive. So, one of the last things she did before we headed out to catch the bus was "dolling" on huge gobs of Wave Set on our hair. Almost immediately the stuff worked like super glue—it kept our hair set but also pasted it to our scalps. The only problem: when we were in PE (physical education) and took showers, the Wave Set turned into goop and poured down over our faces. We had to learn how to keep others from seeing how the greenish stuff flooded our faces, making us look—and feel—like gooey clowns.

One other fresh memory of our schooling in Ritzville was the atmosphere surrounding our classroom. Although grade-schoolers, Dan and I attended class in the high school building and thus were surrounded by junior high-schoolers and even older students. Walking down the hall to the restroom, taking lunch breaks, and even attending other periodic gatherings threw us among more mature groups. It was strange enough for us younger Etulain boys to be catapulted from the almost unique classes in the Lantz School into the Ritzville city schools, but it felt even weirder to be surrounded by so many older students. Elder brother Kenny was there too, although he seemed not to know we existed just down the hall. After all, he was getting old enough to drive, to play football for Ritzville High, and, most excitingly, to date girls.

The decision to sell The Ranch in the summer and fall of 1949 and the quick move to Ellensburg, more than 120 miles to the west, meant we would have to adjust to still another school. And this adjustment was even harder because it was in the middle of October, meaning we were jumping into something already organized and racing ahead. Unwelcome adjustments lurked on the horizon.

6

MAGIC IN RITZVILLE

Transferring to the Ritzville schools in the fall of 1947 added another dimension to our fascination with going to town. Leaving The Ranch and traveling to town was like entering a field of magic for drama-deprived boys.

Saturdays and Sundays proved to be days of adventure—even enchantment—in going to town. Ritzville lay only 22 miles to the west from our sheep ranch, but the one hour trip crossed from one world to another. In our weekly drives toward Ritzville, we passed through Coyote Gulch, over Rock Creek, and near the Harder ranges and also by increasing numbers of wheat fields before traveling down into town. In the winter, some of the gravel and barely oiled roads were slick—and almost dangerous.

When the Etulain family began visiting Ritzville in the late 1930s and early 1940s, the town had established much of its identity. As the county seat, it housed the Adams County Courthouse and the county's main hospital. Its population had boomed to 1,900 in 1920 and then dropped a bit before turning up again. By the early years of the twentieth century, Ritzville had a large reputation as a wheat-shipping site. The Northern Pacific Railway had come to the town in the early 1880s, a key reason for the town's increased shipping prowess. Some said that Ritzville's wheat-shipping totals were among the highest in the nation. Until 1950, it was the largest town between Ellensburg (more than 120 miles to the west) and Spokane (about 60 miles to the northeast). Most of the town's business and future lay in wheat and other grain, but it was a trading center for ranchers as well.

With its population rising from 1,750 to 2,145 during the 1940s, Ritzville seemed like a futuristic world to us rustic Etulain boys. Everything in town was lighted, warmed, and powered by electricity. We could get vehicle servicing at the Chevrolet garage and Walenta's Shell station, and we could tune in to the radio stations whose signal had been unavailable at our ranch house. And there were the post office, the church, the grocery store, and the Ritzville Trading Company, places of fascination that frequently offered services, foods, and goods that we found exotic.

The most important intersection of town was the corner of Division and Main. In the block past Main was the Chevy garage on the left and the post office on the right. At the next intersection, on the right, was the home of our only relatives in Ritzville, the Hebards: Mom's niece Beulah, her husband Frank; and their kids. If we instead turned left at Main, the Safeway grocery store appeared on our left, followed by a delightful bakery and Penney's and the Ritzville Trading Company on the right, while farther down Main lay the doctor's office and the library.

Dad spent much of his Saturday time at Safeway. Sometimes he bought food for up to twenty men. So dependable was his buying that the Safeway people gave him day-old bread to feed the hogs—if he stayed until the store closed that evening. Mom was more likely to go shopping at the clothing or houseware stores or visit the Hebards. We sons, if not forced into piano lessons, headed for the library; or if it was summer or a warm spring or fall day, we zipped up to the park at the top of the hill for its beckoning swimming pool.

The most magical place was the stately antique Carnegie Library. Sent there on Saturday jaunts by our parents while they finished shopping and other weekly tasks, we indulged our curiosity by reading the

The Ritzville Public Library, where Dicky was introduced to the Hardy Boys and Nancy Drew series, the Chip Hilton sports series, and dozens of other books, was a virtual Eden every Saturday.

The Ritzville City Park, where the Etulain family attended Fourth of July picnics and we three boys enjoyed the municipal swimming pool.

The town athletic field, where we watched high school teams and other Ritzville town teams. On the nearby field, we grade-school boys played many a noon keep-away football game. Occasionally, we attended county festivals and enjoyed the snacks and goodies served at those gatherings.

Hardy Boys series, the Chip Hilton series, and other boyhood book fascinations. Bibliomania reigned back then, and still does.

But, ugh, piano lessons also awaited us in Ritzville. Mom believed her sheep-ranch boy rascals needed some culture and that Mrs. Jingling could apply some of the needed refining through weekly piano lessons. When the black-and-white-keys experiment failed terribly, Mom sent us in the direction of other instruments, brother Dan to the clarinet and I to the trumpet. His squeaking and my blatting and our total failures later on with violins finally convinced Mom her experiments in musical culture wouldn't take.

On some Saturdays in town, we got a coveted chance to visit one of Ritzville's handful of restaurants. On one occasion—I think it was at the Circle T eatery—I ordered two hamburgers, which my father wanted to cancel, but Mom said was okay if I ate both. But Dad was right; a bad habit of overeating had begun. We were even served up rabbit several times in a café located on the highway running toward Spokane.

There were a few other usual stops in town. Since we had no refrigerator at home, we depended a good deal on our town locker. I still wince thinking about those really cold times going in with Dad to get the lamb, beef, or pork Mom would roast and put on the table the next week. Sometimes we would make quick stops at the nearby office of the Ritzville *Journal-Times*. Dad was a dedicated newspaper man; newspapers helped him learn to read English, and later he always seemed to have some business with the Ritzville newspaper. And there were the stops at tools and hardware places. Given the size of The Ranch and its incessant demands, we were always in need of new tools or repairs for those that were wearing out.

After these mostly glorious times in town, it was back to The Ranch on late Saturday afternoons. Riding home in our shiny Chevrolet, we boys basked in the magic we had enjoyed.

That Ritzville of our memory shifted dramatically when the I-90 freeway bypassed town, causing those heading east to Spokane or west toward Seattle to seldom enter Ritzville. Losing much of its downtown, businesses relocating elsewhere along the freeway, and its population falling, Ritzville became a different place. I wonder if the town still holds the same magic for boys and girls as it did seventy to eighty years ago for us young, starry-eyed Etulains.

7
GOING TO CHURCH

E very Sunday morning the Etulain family fired up one of its sacred
Chevrolets and headed to church. Our family attended a very
small Church of the Nazarene in Ritzville. We dodged the same
potholes and passed the same coyote dens that were there on Saturday.
These twice-a-week trips to town, except for summer months spent in
Idaho, spread over nearly a dozen years of my life.

My father was born a Roman Catholic in Spain, but, once in the
United States, his brother Juan introduced him, reluctantly at first, to a
Pentecostal church. My mother was the product of another evangelical
denomination, the Mennonite Brethren in Christ. They were newcomers to the Nazarene Church. They had tried the Pentecostal Assembly
of God Church in Ritzville, but that did not work. My father, now a
Protestant, was amenable to Mom's choice of the Nazarene Church.
Over the years, they became increasingly comfortable with the small,
conservative denomination.

Nazarenes were evangelicals but not Fundamentalists. More like
conservative Methodists than enthusiastic Pentecostals, Nazarenes
asked members to read the Bible and follow the teachings of Jesus. But
they were not biblical literalists, and they did not speak in tongues.
Still, their social guidelines were demanding: no alcohol or smoking nor
dancing or movie-going. Despite what the High Church congregants

The Ritzville Church of the Nazarene, our worship place each Sunday morning and sometimes on Sunday nights and during the week. Dad and Mom attended this church for about a dozen years.

of the Catholic, Lutheran, and Congregational denominations might think, we Low Church Nazarenes didn't include "I Want to Be a Jesus Cowboy in the Holy Ghost Corral" or "Dropkick Me Jesus through the Goalposts of Life" in our hymnal. But we did sing enthusiastically, nearly every Sunday, "In My Heart There Rings a Melody" and "I Love to Tell the Story." The musical lessons were clear and explicit for us young guys: Nazarene evangelicals believed in conversion, morality, and hope, and they expected us to follow the rules.

The largest change was in Dad's religious and cultural journey. He became a devoted, loyal Nazarene and encouraged us to join the church. In fact, a different, soft side of Dad emerged in church. Singing favorite hymns—all off-key—like "The Old Rugged Cross" and "No, Never Alone" brought tears to his eyes. And he could not testify (speak up) in church without choking up with emotion. Before long, Dad's church decision kept him out of typical Basque cultural gatherings. No alcohol or dancing; that was a shift away from his heritage. A Basque Nazarene was a cultural oxymoron.

We three Etulain boys, rapscallions of the first order, kept things lively in Sunday School. We tried to sit still through "Opening Exercises" and class sessions, but activity times and outings offered more entertainment than preachy Bible lessons. We enjoyed our Sunday School teacher Buff Oldridge, though; he even piled us into the back of his pickup and took us to the amusement park or car races in Spokane.

Like other kids attending the Nazarene church, we attempted to hide out in the back seats during morning services, away from our parents' looks and gestures. On a few embarrassing occasions, when we had been acting up in some way they noticed, Mom or Dad would get up from the front of the church (they always sat in the second or third row), come back and get us, and take us back to sit us next to them, near the altar.

Piano music, a vocal solo, a prayer, and the pastor's seemingly endless sermons were a tiresome schedule for pre-teen boys. But whenever a contest was held to find the correct Bible verse, we were all in for the competition, usually knowing where the verse was hidden among the sixty-six books.

Sometimes a snack between Sunday School and church service kept us half alive, and at the end of the two hours we were zipping back to The Ranch. We knew a big dinner of roast lamb was near at hand when the Old-Fashioned Revival Hour blared on the radio as we drove home.

Those early years at Ritzville's Nazarene church had a lasting effect on us Etulain boys. Brother Ken went to a Nazarene high school in Nampa, Idaho, and Dan and I attended and graduated from Northwest Nazarene College (now a university). Later, Dan and I taught at the college in Nampa. I have attended a Nazarene church all my life, teaching Sunday School classes for more than fifty years and serving on church boards for more than forty years.

In some ways, the Nazarene experiences were even more life changing for Dad. Becoming an evangelical separated him from his Basque
and Catholic cultures. Once he converted to Protestantism, he rarely
attended Basque gatherings and gave up alcohol. Yet a commitment
to church carried over from his own early to later years. A Catholic
church-going youth became a Nazarene-going adult. His denomination might have changed but not his dedication to church things,
including consistent attendance, abundant giving, and an emotional
attachment to Christianity.

8

HERDERS
AND HIRED MEN

E ven before Dan and I were aware of such things, Dad was hiring
an expanding core of herders and hired men. Shortly after Dad
and Uncle Juan divided their sheep in 1936, Dad began running
7,000–8,000 ewes and their lambs and a few bucks on his ranch. That
meant he needed at least four separate bands to accommodate that
many sheep. Indeed, when lambing time came (January–March), his
workforce ballooned to as many as twenty men. In addition, he always
had at least one hired man, usually accompanied by his family, living
in the hired man's house, near the Etulain home.

Dad tried to hire Basque herders as often as he could, confident
of their diligence, dependability, and durability. But the availability
of Basque herders was uncertain in the 1920s and 1930s. The US
Congress, under pressure from anti-assimilationist conservatives,
passed legislation in the early 1920s that severely limited immigration,
even from countries like Spain and France. That meant that Spanish
and French Basque herders could come only in miniscule numbers.
Over time, pressure from ranchers and congressmen in sheep-raising
states brought about special legislation that allowed more Basque
herders to immigrate to the United States. These enactments resulted

largely from two trends: (1) not many American men wanted to take on a low-paying, taxing, and negatively imaged occupation like sheepherding; and (2) on the positive side, Basques had gained an undeserved but attractive reputation as the best and most-experienced shepherds in Europe and the American West. When Dad could do so, he hired Basques first of all. He preferred not to hire American men because he thought too many had turned out to be undependable for the hard, demanding work of sheepherding.

Sheepherding is a difficult, lonesome kind of work, a daylight-to-dusk occupation. The herders at our ranch also had to live apart from other people, including their wife or children. Indeed, we had no available living space for married herders at our ranch, and we did not house them in the bunkhouse. Herders had to be out in the pastures with their bands. Our herders lived in small, decrepit cabins scattered across The Ranch; they lacked running water or bathrooms. If no cabins were available, the herders resided in tents. They were also expected to serve as lay veterinarians, taking care of the needs of their ewes and lambs. In addition, they had to protect the sheep from the ever-present coyotes that were bent on eating mutton for dinner. Although I did not realize in my boyhood years why so few wanted to work as sheepherders, it became clear later on that the work was too arduous, isolated, and low paying to attract many men.

Of our Basque herders, I remember most Serviano Galeneña. Dad spoke as highly of him as any of our herders. Soft-spoken, gentle, and dependable in all ways, Serviano lived up to the high level of performance that Dad expected of Basque herders. The problem was that his wife did not enjoy the isolated living on our distant ranch. And for some reason, their son, Jimmy, and I clashed. In our several tussles, he usually pummeled me more than I could handle. Serviano did not stay as long as Dad would have liked because of the unhappiness of his family.

There was also "Shorty," never known by any other name among us. Built like a fireplug (similar to Dad), Shorty exuded energy and

Dad (left) as a camptender and Uncle Juan (right) as a herder.

Mom's nephew Manly Gillard as an Etulain ranch worker.

decisiveness. Even his walk told onlookers he was in charge and could take on anything asked of him. Dad depended on Shorty to get his bands through demanding circumstances with minimal losses.

On one occasion, I may have gotten Mom and Dad in trouble with one of our herders. Bill Ledford was a talker, someone who let you know what he thought ought to be done. We were talking with him

Tents on the Etulain ranch for herders and hired men in the 1930s.

in one of the sheep camps when Bill blurted out one of his opinions. And I, probably not more than five or six, fired back, "Oh, Bill, you are nothing but a windbag." He spun around and looked at Mom and Dad, as if to say, "Well, I know what you're saying about me at your house." Bill did not stay much longer; he went over to Sunnyside to work for Uncle Juan.

Johnny Jacobs, Leon Zocolo, Anton Onderland, Jack Echart, and Felix(?) Zozaya were other herders. I don't recall much about them, save that Dad liked having Basques like Leon and Jack work for him as long as they could. Johnny, a long, lean, and soft-spoken man, tied himself to the Etulain family in a special way. Johnny and his wife had trouble living together, so their son, little Johnny, came to live with his father on The Ranch. Mom did a good deal of "Moming" for little Johnny. He often stayed at our house, and for a short period of time he went to the Lantz School with us. A warmed-hearted, gregarious little guy, he seemed like our little brother, whom we much enjoyed.

One family had a rather unique connection with The Ranch. The Allegrias had a home in Sprague, about twenty miles northeast of The Ranch. They were Spanish, not Basque, but fit in very well with the local Basques. Father Bacillio Allegria worked for us for long periods of time, more as a ranch hand than a herder. Mrs. Allegria, an enthusiastic cook, expertly operated the cookshack and prepared huge meals at lambing and shearing times. We remember her enormous servings of lamb, grilled lamb fries, and washbasins of tapioca, and eagerly referring to all of them as "muy gooz," her translation of "very good." Daughter Margarita helped her in the cookhouse, and their son, Tony, held essential jobs—like shoveling the manure out of the loafing sheds. We were good friends with the Allegrias, even going to Sprague to watch the Catholic High School play that featured the Allegria kids.

A few relatives came to The Ranch to take on one or two of the several home-based jobs Dad had available. Two of Mom's nephews, Manly and Lowell Gillard—sons of two of her brothers—worked at The Ranch for a short while in their twenties, before they married. Both seemed to get along with Dad and in late life spoke very positively about their experiences at the Etulain ranch.

In addition to the herders and other ranch workers, Dad always had a full-time hired man, but usually no more than one. The assignments for the hired men differed from those of herders. The hired men who lived at the home place were in charge of cow miking (sometimes five to ten cows) and other such ranch duties as feeding sheep in the corrals, hauling hay out to the sheep bands in the pastures, and helping to unload the hay-hauling and feed trucks that came to The Ranch quite often.

Hired men rarely worked in the pastures with sheep, while herders infrequently worked at the home place. The hired men and their families lived in the rather ramshackle hired-man's house. The Sextons were the first such family I remember, with their son, Darrell, being a buddy of Ken's. Their family also had a special-needs little girl who demanded almost full-time care. The Criders, who came next, were from New Mexico. Mr. Crider served as our taxi back and forth to the Lantz School. They stayed only about one year before moving on.

The one hired-man's family I remember the most and the one our family was especially close to was the Brooks. A young and newly married couple, Don and Jolene Brooks answered Dad's advertisement for a hired man in the *Spokesman-Review* (Spokane). Barely out of high school, they moved down to the Etulain ranch for their first job. They were from Colville, where both had been raised. Donny (or Danny), a quiet guy, did his job well, which included milking up to a half-dozen or more cows morning and night and preparing the milk for their and our houses, for the hogs, and for sale. He also did a good deal of driving and delivering on The Ranch, where we were now raising more cows than sheep. Jolene, a tall, amiable woman, quickly became friends with everyone. She was particularly intelligent and insightful. We kids delighted in going over to the Brooks house to play spirited games of Monopoly or Rook. By background Seventh-Day Adventists, Don and Jolene began attending and became solid members of the Ritzville Nazarene Church. Undoubtedly, seeing them in our church each Sunday cemented a tighter familial friendship than those we had with prior hired men's families. Our connections continued with the Brookses well after both families left The Ranch in 1949.

For me and my brothers, the herders and hired men and their families were people who enlarged our otherwise provincial experiences. The personalities of the herders, the kids of the hired men, and the hired men themselves gave us a sense of a wider world than one based on only our household.

9

LAMBING SEASON

Family planning among the woolies began in early fall. Once the ewes were back on the ranch after spending the summer months in the mountains, the bucks/rams were turned in with the ewes. This togetherness usually lasted from mid-September, at the earliest, until toward the end of October. Enthusiastic breeding followed, and sheep families were soon on their way.

The gestation period of ewes and the needs of the market determined breeding schedules among our sheep. We wanted lambs born in the January–March period so the marketable lambs could be ready for sale in the early fall during the Jewish High Holidays. Since the normal time for ewes to carry lambs is four to five months, and we wanted those lambs ready for market in September or October of the next fall, that meant most lambs needed to be born in the dead of winter, January–February. Scheduling lambing season for the coldest, snowiest time of the year seemed unwise, but birth cycles and especially meeting the best-selling season were more influential than the weather in our decision-making.

At first, Dad favored the Hampshire breed for his bucks, but then he changed his mind and gradually shifted to raising black-faced Suffolk. He had earlier purchased Hampshires because of their luxuriant wool, but as World War II shifted industry interests away from wool and toward synthetics such as rayon and nylon, Dad abandoned the wool-rich Hampshire breed for what he considered the more prolific Suffolk. His dream was 100 percent or more production, meaning that his ewes would average at least one lamb each. He was convinced that his Suffolk ewes, by bearing more twins, came much closer to that reproductive goal than the Hampshires.

Once lambing season began, soon after the first of the year, schedules for herders and other ranch workers had to be adjusted. Lambing weeks were the most labor-intensive time of the year. Dad hired as many as twenty men to help with lambing. As many pregnant ewes as possible were brought in close to the home place, where their birthing challenges could be more readily addressed than farther out on the open range. Having so many expectant ewes and their soon-to-arrive offspring crowding our home ranch meant setting up new procedures.

Dad hired at least one night man so that the lambing corral was looked after around the clock. At the northern end of the corral, the small enclosure for the night watchman included a bed, a small stove, and lambing supplies. Every hour, lantern in hand, the night man checked the ewes corralled or nearby, looking for any newly born lambs, and taking the new mothers and their offspring to smaller catch pens at the covered, protected edge of the corral. Each ewe was given extra feed and water, but her stay with her new lamb in the catch pen was short because other new arrivals quickly needed the pens.

Of course, not all the lambing went smoothly. Unexpected challenges and even full-blown tragedies invaded the scene. Some of the ewes, especially the first-time mothers, had difficulty with the birthing process. More than a few times in a twenty-four-hour period the nighttime or daytime lambing workers had to help. For pre-teen boys seeing their father or another man up to his elbow inside a ewe trying to ensure a successful birth (occasionally by turning around an unborn lamb) was a sometimes-disturbing sight. But the workers had to be ready for such lamb-birthing scenarios.

Lambing time in the corrals.

Lamb maternity ward in the fields.

Even those life-saving attempts did not protect all the ewes and lambs. In fact, lambing season often spawned a mushrooming orphanage as well as a burgeoning contingent of lambless ewes, when either the mothers or lambs expired in the birthing process. Again, new processes had to be quickly put into effect. When a ewe died but her lamb or twins survived, surrogate mothers had to be found. That was not an easy process because many ewes without lambs had no milk, and those with lambs were often hesitant to take on new little ones that did not smell like their own. Some of the ewes were so offensive in their actions that they had to be tied to the side of the catch pen fence to enable the hungry orphans to nurse from them.

More often, the process meant transitioning a newly orphaned lamb from its motherless status to a ewe who had lost her own lamb. To make this unusual process work best, Dad turned to what he called the "jacketing." He or one of the herders would skin the newly deceased lamb and put the skin on the orphan and in the process spread as much of the smell of the dead lamb on the orphan so the ewe might accept the motherless little one because it now smelled like her own lamb.

But when these and other processes did not work, we ended up with a large pen of orphans or "bummers" (bottle-fed lambs). Sometimes the orphan pen held two or three dozen hungry, bleating lambies. It was a sight to see the night or day lambing man holding two ketchup-sized bottles (or larger) with nipples on the end headed to the bummer quarters. Often, we Etulain boys were called in to help with this time-consuming process. The bummers, soon recognizing the bottle holders, pushed or butted at them and "baaed" out their hunger pangs. Even after some of the orphans had been in the bummer pen for several days, we tried to adopt them to ewes who had lost their own lambs. That adopting process rarely worked quickly or smoothly.

The bummer-feeder journey sometimes continued in an unplanned sequence. When the orphan lambs grew up to be sturdy females and looked like good candidates for motherhood, they were kept through their first months and then sometimes bred as early as the next fall— although most at a later time. But the bummers remembered their infant feeding routines. Sometimes, even after they had become mothers themselves, they hung around the feeding pen or near the back door of our house if that was where they were fed as bums. They never forgot the special treatment they got, the rich milk they loved, and the attention they had received at these sites. It was not unusual for a young mother to brush up against someone near the feeding pen or back doorstep, acting out their memories of previous special treatment.

Lambing season was the launching stage for lambs, leading to their short life from birth to death. In January or February they were newly born ones trying to fend off cold, hunger, and sometimes estrangement. By March, if an early spring came, they might be out frolicking in pastures that were beginning to green up.

Before shearing time in April or May, our lambs went through a traumatic process. Docking and "cutting" times are seared into my memory. Lambs were docked to ward off possible infections at their tail ends. We boys often played a part in this repugnant but necessary procedure. A standard process was followed. We grabbed lambs that had been brought into a small pen, gathered their left front and back feet in our left hand and their right front and back feet in our right hand. Then we lifted the lambs waist-high to a 1" x 10" or 1" x 8" board placed flat on mid-height posts, exposing their back ends to Dad, the herders, or the hired men on the other side of the fence. Taking a hot iron from a nearby fire, the men burned through the lamb's tail, leaving only a stub. For male lambs there was further agony. Grabbing a male's scrotum, the herders cut off its end, pinched down the testicles, and pulled them out with their teeth, before dropping them in a nearby bucket. For those wishing to enjoy such delicacies, lamb fries (or some called them "Basque beans") were grilled that night for supper.

The next three or four days were tough times for lambs suffering from docking and cutting. Their bleatings were often heard. Later, sheepmen used an elastrator (like a tough, large rubber band) and placed it around the head of the scrotum, cutting off the circulation and allowing the scrotum eventually to dry up and drop off. This procedure prevented infections from developing, the kind that earlier methods of cuttings often brought on. Curiously, I flinch less about the cutting process than the docking of tails when a lamb was suffering from "scours" (diarrhea). The stench generated from the iron in that mess was so strong that I still recall it seventy years later. These were not looked-forward-to times for lambies or ranch boys.

10

THE SHEEPSHEARERS ARE COMING

They came like a cavalcade of motorized wagons headed west. Except they weren't newcomers on the Oregon Trail but sheepshearers in their trucks, campers, and jerry-built contraptions. Most came north from the Southwest for their annual work week at our ranch.

The arrival of the sheepshearers signaled upcoming days of arduous work—for everyone. More than 7,000 sheep had to be sheared in dirty, backbreaking labor.

Our sheepshearing shed stood less than a mile north from our ranch home. The sheep were brought in from the pastures and crowded into large pens that connected, through narrow alleyways, to the back side of the shearing shed. Hanging canvas strips served as dividers between the alleyways and the shearers, keeping the sheep at bay until a shearer reached out to grab the next reluctant woolie. Quickly turning the captured sheep on its tail end, the shearer cut off the front and back of last year's wool coat. In three minutes or less, the sheep was shorn and pushed out the front side of the shearing shed—to join the other bleating, dazed, four-legged ones out there.

The shearing crew at work. *1986-27-43. "Sheep." Bureau of Reclamation, Montour Project Collection. Idaho State Archives.*

The shearing routine at our place demanded nearly a week of bone-wearying work. The company of shearers working in the bays of our shearing shed, laboring at top speed for eight hours (not many could do this, however), sheared about 1,500–1,600 sheep a day, or more than 7,000 in five days. The shearers brought with them a truck with a gas-fired engine on its bed to run the up-to-date shearing tools each of the shearers wielded. A series of metal rods connected all the shearing shed bays, in which each shearer worked with a shearing machine that resembled a clackety skeleton de-wooling an endless string of sheep.

If the shearers were all-day workhorses, the energetic and mischievous ranch boys still found ways to engage with them, sometimes not by choice on either end. Men who bunched up the shorn wool and carried it to a long wool sack (about eight feet long), hanging at the end of the shed, loved to grab one of the owner's sons and toss him down into it. There was no way out until he was rescued. At first it seemed fun, but Mom hated our lanolin-soaked clothes and detested the creepy, crawly critters that often migrated from the wool bundles onto our bodies.

Then, at night we would sneak out of the house and over to one of the campers or homemade truck wagons to join the shearers and their families. For girl-starved ranch rascals there were the shearers' daughters and new boy chums arriving that week; the evening visits were also relished experiences. One memorable occasion featured a noted raconteur among the shearers telling a dramatic, mysterious story in his camper about a man who had a golden arm that had been stolen. Asking repeatedly in a soft voice, "I wonder who has it" and "Do you have it," he suddenly burst into a thunderous "You've got it" and simultaneously leaped threateningly toward us. Wet pants—maybe.

The shearing process at our ranch illustrated a step forward in spring shearing. Early in the twentieth century, sheepmen took their flocks to a central shearing place. For example, the town of Sprague, about twenty miles from our ranch, was once a shearing spot for nearby sheepmen. Because it was an expensive, time-consuming process to trail sheep to these shearing spots, ranchers often stopped at a place like Sprague for shearing on their way to nearby mountain pastures for summer grazing. But Dad realized that he needed something different, as did most nearby sheepmen. Most larger sheep-ranch owners thus started erecting their own shearing sheds.

Toward the end of the week, with dozens of tightly packed wool sacks stacked near the shearing shed, we jumped around on them. Games of tag were de rigueur when the stacked wool sacks mounted up.

Once shearing was completed, the stuffed wool sacks were trucked to the nearby siding at Paxson on the Milwaukee Road. That was a time-consuming trip since not many of the huge wool sacks could be loaded on our regular-sized Chevy truck. On a few occasions, another trucker, sometimes with a truck and trailer, would load up our wool and take the bulging sacks to markets. Even some shipments were made south to the Pendleton Woolen Mills in Pendleton, Oregon. More often, our wool went east by rail on the Milwaukee Road.

Loading the full wool sacks for the trip to market.

Dad marking a full wool sack.

The week of the shearers at The Ranch was a much-anticipated part of our social calendar. The shearers and their families brought new life every spring.

Shearing was also a tense time. After all, much of Dad's revenue as a sheepman came from wool sales. Through World War II, wool sales competed with lamb sales to line Dad's pockets.

11

TRAILING—ON THE ROAD TO IDAHO

A few days after shearing was finished and the plump, stuffed wool sacks were off the scene, Dad geared up to send a band of sheep trailing across eastern Washington and into the Idaho mountains near the Montana border. It was a grueling trip for the 1,500–2,000 ewes and their lambs. The band would have to cover nearly 300 miles of trailing in a month.

During this procedure, we carried out what anthropologists call "transhumance." We were moving our livestock from one kind of pasture—lower ranch—to another kind of grazing—upper mountain. It was a form of pastoral nomadism.

We ranch sons knew less about the trailing month of May because we were not involved. Ken might have taken part, although school was still on, blocking out weekdays. Sundays were out, but we did travel with Dad once or twice during his weekly trips to check on and resupply the trailers.

Dad assembled a travel group to chauffeur the band of 3,000–4,000 sheep (ewes and lambs) along the backroads of eastern Washington, into Idaho, and up the western slopes of the Bitterroot Mountains east of St. Maries. Usually, at least two men—sometimes one or two more—were assigned to the trailing band. One man with a bellwether or ewe headed up the nomads, hoping that the sheep, as per usual, would trek after the leader. A second herder brought up the rear of the band. Accompanying the band was a sheep wagon pulled by horses or, more likely, a pickup pulling the camp wagon. The wagon provided overnight and cooking accommodations for the herders and was usually packed full of supplies for the men involved. If a pickup pulled the sheep wagon, it too was loaded with supplies. All the way along to Idaho, a half-dozen dogs were central to the success of the trailing, often barking at the recalcitrant and errant ewes.

The trailing band, usually consisting of the oldest lambs on The Ranch and only ewes with single lambs (no twins), headed east, trying as much as possible to stay out of towns. That was rarely possible. In fact, the yearly trailings east were but another sign of our close ties to the Palouse Country. The route usually led through or near Ewan, St. John, Thornton, and Oakesdale in Washington and through or by De Smet and Santa in Idaho. Next, the band headed on northeast to just east of St. Maries but near the St. Joe River and up to Calder. Then the trailed sheep were situated near one of Dad's sheep camps scattered from Calder to Herrick.

Several worrisome challenges faced the trailers. The most notable of these was keeping to the schedule. The sheep needed daily food and water for the next twenty to thirty days. Dad thus hoped both were easily available each day. If not, he and his bands were in trouble. His yearly plan included stocking up on the needed supplies, while grazing lands were secured all along the trip. Some grain was carried by the travelers or came to them via Dad's frequent visits. But weather conditions, changing owners, and road conditions could wreak havoc with his well-planned schedule. Since Dad was unavailable for the most part and cell phones—in fact any kind of phone—were not at hand, herders often had to make spur-of-the-moment decisions to adjust to schedule shifts.

Dealing with cars and trucks attempting to pass through the trailing band was another perplexing challenge. Too often, drivers,

Trailing sheep often left incriminating evidence.

Sheep trailers tried to avoid towns by moving their bands to the mountains. They hoped to find out-of-the-way country roads for their trailing paths. *1978-37-100f. "Sheepherder and Flock." Idaho Association of Commerce and Industry Collection. Idaho State Archives.*

unaccustomed to how sheep reacted, didn't move quietly through the band but blared their horns repeatedly, alarming the already jumpy woolies. The herders tried to keep this upset from occurring by speaking to drivers before they entered the band or frequently leading the cars through the band with the help of their dogs.

Other challenges faced the trailers in towns. Most town dwellers did not like having sheep or cattle move through their streets because they notoriously left evidence of their having traversed the area. Certainly sheep left their droppings. But the town ordinances in Washington and Idaho allowed our bands to move, expeditiously, through the streets—if the travel was well-conducted. Still, townies hated having to clean up after the sheep relieved themselves on the streets.

Dad never made entirely clear why he sent one band up the road and shipped the other two or three by rail. Was it the need to get started with the older lambs? Was it less expensive to trail than to ship a band? Did he need to get part of the sheep off The Ranch as early as possible because of the dwindling supply of grazing grass? Or were there other reasons? Whatever Dad's thinking on the matter, he loaded the other bands around the first of June at the Paxson siding of the Milwaukee Road just to the east of our ranch boundary. In a matter of a few hours, all the bands—the trailers and those by rail—were joined at the Calder or Herrick drop-offs, ready for a summer of healthy grazing on abundant grasses on the western slopes of the Bitterroot Mountains.

Summer had begun.

12

SUMMERS IN ST. MARIES

We lived summers in St. Maries from before my recall through the early fall of 1944. After that and once Dad began to cut down on his sheep ranching and replace his sheep with more cattle, we did not need to take our smaller bands of sheep to the mountains for summer grazing.

When Dad first began taking his own sheep to the mountains between Calder and Herrick, Idaho, he was building on family tradition. In fact, he may even have herded some of his uncle Martin's sheep in the Bitterroot Mountains before having his own sheep. Dad's older brother, Uncle Juan, also began to take his sheep to the mountains near St. Maries about the same time as Dad.

Our modest house in St. Maries, located at 332 South 11th Street on a hill two or three blocks south of Main Street, was our home for three to four months each summer. The rest of the year it was rented out. When we arrived, Dad and Mom spent a good deal of time and energy cleaning up after the renters and filling the basement back-in area with supplies for sheep camps in the mountains. Dad's pickup was often backed down to this basement area and loaded with food for the herders and dogs.

The Etulain summer home in St. Maries, Idaho, from the 1930s until 1944–45.

The trips up to the mountains to contact the herders of the three to four bands occurred every week, sometimes more than once each week. There were six to eight men with the three or four bands, and a total of as many as fifteen to twenty dogs. It was about 25 miles from St. Maries to Calder, via the St. Joe River Road or Forest Highway 50. Dad crossed the St. Joe River at Calder and drove another eight miles on the North Side Road along the St. Joe over to Herrick. Usually the herder or more likely the camptender brought down the packhorses and mules at the agreed-upon time, and Dad transferred the week's supplies from his pickup to the worker, who returned to his band with the stores. The three to four bands totaled anywhere from 6,000 to 8,000 sheep plus an equal number of lambs. The land Dad used for grazing, some owned and some rented, stretched from Calder and Herrick. Traveling between these two towns, neither of which boasted 100 residents, we crossed over Elk Creek and came to Big Creek on the western edge of Herrick. Dad's bands moved about a good deal in the summer but remained in the mountains to the north of the St. Joe River. Often our main stop would be a thrown-together cabin near Herrick, where the mice and pack rats for most of the year took up residence when herders were not there.

Our neighbors in St. Maries included a local luminary or two. Just down and across the street in front of our house was the attractive brick home of Dr. C. A. Robins at 245 South 11th Street. He was our family doctor. He took out our tonsils and fed us soft cold ice cream to calm the upset. Dr. Robins became active in local politics, grew known in northern Idaho, and was elected Idaho governor from 1947 to 1951. He was a staunch Republican, making him all the more laudable to my died-in-the-wool Republican parents. Across the alley from our back door was the Critzer family. Mr. Critzer was known throughout St. Maries as the leading train wrecker operator on the Milwaukee Road railroad that was so important to the town—and to the Etulains.

On one unusual day, the phone rang in our summer home in St. Maries. When Mom answered, the caller's voice blurted out, "Your boys are down here in the main street without their clothes. Are they trying to be nudists?" Well, Mom remembered that story ever after. She told it again and again. It happened in our preschool days—earlier than our memories stretch back to.

As we got older, Mom, very busy as usual, allowed her three sons to roam around St. Maries. We hung out down on the docks of the St. Joe River, frequented the swimming pool in the park about five blocks away, ganged up with the neighborhood Osure and Demichael guys as often as we could. On our way down to feast on ice cream at the Handi Corner on Main Street we would sometimes visit upon others our youthful, religious bias. Passing the Catholic school, we would yell out at the "Catlickers," and they would yell back, "Doglickers."

Our days and weeks in St. Maries were usually ones of leisure—fun, mainly. Since we were not on The Ranch, needed chores were not looming, and Dad seemed too busy to find something for us to do. So, off we went, to the swimming holes, running with chums, and haunting the downtown area. Sundays, of course, were church days—at the very small, rustic Church of the Nazarene down the street from us. Some of my earliest St. Maries memories were crying about something in the earth-surrounded basement of Sunday School classes. Equally

Heyburn Elementary School in St. Maries, where the Etulain boys attended from the late 1930s until 1944.

early were the vague memories of walking down the street with Mom and Danny to the nursery school and other preschools.

On a few occasions, we got out of town. One of our favorite outings was a Sunday afternoon picnic on the shores of Lake Coeur d'Alene a few miles north of St. Maries. At the Rocky Point beach, Mom unpacked a big lunch and Dad snoozed under the shade trees while we boys got into water fights along and around the docks. Sometimes we ventured a bit farther north and turned in at Chatcolet for other beach adventures. Even less frequently, we would drive a few miles south of St. Maries to visit Uncle Juan and Aunt Margaret—before they were blessed with two daughters, Bonita and Arnola.

Summers in St. Maries ended in rush. Up at Herrick, Dad loaded up the lambs, wethers (castrated males), and older and barren ewes on the Milwaukee Road, boarded the train, and headed for Chicago. Along the way, Dad and other sheepmen played a game with buyers, hoping to win the game. In a stop in Aberdeen, South Dakota, the sheepmen loaded up their animals with water, hoping that it would increase the total weight of the sheep by the first market stop at the Twin Cities in Minnesota. But the buyers knew the old trick. They ran the for-sale sheep around the sale yards until the excess liquid was lost one way or another. If the market prices were low in the Twin Cities, Dad and his sheep continued on to the historic Union Stockyards in Chicago. He was stuck with whatever the market would bear in Chicago to sell his sheep. He would go no farther east.

His return was a big deal for the Etulains. Down to the St. Maries railroad station we went to celebrate upon his arrival. He had promised, for the future, that as soon as we were old enough, he would take us on the trip east with the sheep. Sadly, things changed in the sheep-raising world, and the trip never happened.

Even before Dad returned from selling his sheep, we would begin packing. Soon all of us, with the car and pickup loaded, would be heading back to The Ranch in the eastern Washington outback. The summer town guys were again returning to the range country.

13

A PASSEL OF SHEEPDOGS

Our pack of sheepdogs, numbering at least twenty and sometimes more, was a much-valued segment of The Ranch operation. Open-range sheep raising with large bands demanded trained dogs to aid in herding the sheep and warding off pesky predators. The four-footed fidos also became appreciated companions for herders and other ranch workers—and for the Etulain family.

Dad never cared much about the breed of his dogs. Other sheepmen, especially the Basques, might insist on one of the gigantic Pyrenees dogs from Basque country. Still others might prefer Old English sheepdogs or Australian shepherds. But not Dad. The ranch dogs he wanted were those that could learn their assignments and work well with herders on the ranges, near the home place, or in the mountains. He also wasn't particular about their breeding. Indeed, Dad rarely said anything about the pedigree of his sheepdogs.

Usually, four or five dogs were allotted to each herder and his band of up to 2,000 ewes and sometimes equal numbers of lambs in the spring. The largest challenge in this herder-canine relationship was for a herder to teach his nimble helpers the meanings of his words and his hand signals. For instance, the herder might yell out, "Hey, Bob, way

Dad with his beloved sheepdogs.

A herder-camptender in the Idaho mountains with
his two dogs.

round, way round," indicating simultaneously with words and circling gestures that he wanted his dogs to circle his band. Or, the herder's shrill whistle could gain the attention of his dogs, followed by hand signals indicating what actions he wished. Often, dogs crouched in expectation as they waited for the herder's directions.

Pushy dogs often worked like agents of magic in aiding herders. Sheep were often notoriously skittish followers. Scare a ewe, have her take off, and the whole band might immediately go on the run—in the wrong, dangerous direction. On occasion, however, the frenzied relationship seemed to work out well. If a herder had a malleable, dependable bellwether or ewe, he could utilize either to keep his band on track or on trail.

But spooky sheep and the bands often spiraled out of control. Dependable dogs were invaluable on these occasions. Barked herder directions and clear hand signals directed the veteran canines to head off and round up a band running in the wrong direction. On more than a few occasions, dogs saved one of our bands from danger or destruction.

Dad's dogs assisted in several other needy situations. When herders were attempting to push the sheep into a railroad car, up a chute, or from one field to another, dogs nimbly aided their efforts by nipping at the heels of slowpokes or by pushing alongside them. And if dangerous coyotes slunk onto the scene, some of the sufficiently courageous dogs darted forward, snarling and barking, often causing the predators to turn tail.

After nearly seventy years, some individual ranch dogs remain etched in my memory. Banjo was a warm-hearted, loyal helper of herder and yardman Serviano. Bob was every person's lively favorite, a black-and-white racer, jumping to catch and return anything thrown in his direction—for another fetch game. Our little brown-and-white house dog, Tuffy, older brother Kenny's companion, loved to take part in dogfights—at a distance. Once other dogs rushed into a vicious conflict near the dog pens or out toward the center of the home place,

Tuffy would sneak up to the edge of the fighters, bite an exposed hind leg, then scurry back and growl and snarl like the fighter he was not. Later, Old "Maan" (as Dad called him), became my father's ever-present companion. Resting under the front porch, he bounced into action when Dad came outside, grabbed his shovel and boots, and headed out to irrigate or look over the fields. Old Man remained at his heels until they returned.

Moose was an unforgettable ranch dog. We boys called his breed "radar dogs" because their long hair hung over their eyes in such bundles that we wondered if they could see. One incident illustrated Moose's near-blindness. When a cottontail rabbit cautiously moved out of a pile of rubbish, Moose spied the hopper and went after him in a flash. The rabbit, fleeing for life, dashed quickly into a nearby post pile. Evidently not seeing the pile of posts, Moose hit the stack at full tilt. He survived but not without injured pride and a sore face.

Sometimes our herders, exhibiting what they thought to be a sense of humor, used shears to shave dogs like Moose of their abundant hair, turning them into spiffy poodles. For most dogs like Moose, it was embarrassing. They slunk off in their near nakedness, disappearing for days at a time.

From early spring until early winter, the dogs were kept in action, whether at the home ranch, on the trail to the mountains, or in the mountains. Doggie duties at The Ranch and the trail work were famil-iar obligations for the trained dogs, but in the mountains new and dangerous opponents quickly came on the scene. Just as our bands arrived in the mountains east of St. Maries and near the St. Joe River in late May or early June, hibernating bears were emerging from their long slumbers. They were very hungry. The hairy, ravenous beasts, unlike many Americans, liked lamb and mutton—or seemed to. When the newly arrived sheep wandered into the bears' domains, promising four-legged meals were at hand.

As the bears headed toward the sheep, our dogs showed their mettle and, sometimes, or not, their experience. Herders were not reluctant to use their dogs—and guns—to keep the destructive bears away from their sheep bands. Indeed, so widespread were bear attacks on summering sheep that game wardens looked the other way when herders shot down any of the hairy beasts invading the scene. Often, at the behest of herders, their dogs dashed toward the bears, barking and yelping. Veteran and rookie dogs quickly exhibited their experiential differences in these tense moments. The seasoned dogs knew, from past similar incidents, not to get too close to their large opponents. These dogs barked, growled, and acted violently by dashing toward the bears but quickly jumping back when the bears moved threateningly toward them. Unfortunately, and often tragically, the rookies lacked the life-saving strategies. The newcomers would go after the bears, courageous certainly but also displaying their foolhardiness. When they got too close, bears, with a vicious swing of their paws, could dash the life from these innocents abroad. Nearly every year, at least one or two of the new and young dogs lost their lives during these close, violent encounters. If they survived, they returned the next year to the mountains less foolish and more cautious for any future combat with bears.

These bear-dog battles took place in the Idaho mountains about 200–300 miles from our home ranch and nearly thirty miles east of our summer home in St. Maries. Another kind of battle, sometimes even more vicious and certainly more fratricidal, occurred at our home ranch. Our dogs, penned up since the end of the year—to keep them from becoming a wild, dangerous pack of dogs attacking sheep or the animals of our neighbors—were let out in early spring. Chaos followed. Those dogs who felt themselves leaders of the pack thought it necessary to reaffirm their dominion. Other dogs wanted to challenge the old dogs—and did so. A violent dogfight (and sometimes more than one) ensued over leadership. Even though ranch hands tried to quell them, the murderous fighting usually led to a dog death or two every spring.

Another challenge came on the scene in the late 1940s toward the end of our stay at The Ranch. After World War II, it was increasingly difficult for Dad to secure Basque herders, his first choice to work his sheep bands. When their supply dried up, Dad had to turn to American herders. They were not a promising source and their hiring did not work out well. Most ranch workers disliked the isolated, low-paying work of herding sheep when compared with punching cattle or doing other ranch work and farm work. That meant Dad rarely found first-rate American herders once he could no longer count on his much-preferred Basque shepherds. A further challenge came when these new herders tried to work with herd dogs who had learned commands, words, and hand signals in another language. The essence of the problem, of course, was that our dogs were not bilingual; they could not switch easily and quickly from Basque to English.

14

OTHER ANIMALS

Aside from the thousands of sheep and cattle and the dozens of dogs that inhabited our ranch, other animals were important to us. Some were helpful; others proved nasty predators.

Many ranches and ranchers often relied heavily on horses. We did not, even though we did have a few horses—and sometimes mules—on site. I think we shied away from horses because of Dad. I do not ever recall—not once—seeing Dad on a horse. Probably his short, stocky body kept him from being comfortable on most horses. His legs would not have fit well into most stirrups, and he likely would have bounced more in the saddle than was comfortable. Besides, Dad believed he could take a pickup into or through any place a horseman could. And for the most part, he did. That's why many of our pickups needed so much repair at the Chevy garage in Ritzville and lasted such short times.

But other ranch inhabitants felt otherwise. Horses were most needed during the summer when we moved sheep bands in the mountains. Packhorses were the primary means of transportation in moving from one camp location to another and hauling in supplies for the sheep and herders. Some of our hired men and their families and brother Ken wanted riding horses; sometimes even a herder or two wanted to use them. And in a few unusual situations, we needed horses to pull a

At first Dad rode horses as a herder; later, his hard-working Chevy pickups served in place of horses.

ranch contraption. So, we kept a few horses, some for packing, some for riding, and others for ranch work, in a horse corral.

Dad did not enjoy cats, at least not house cats. But they were often in residence anyway, in the milking parlor and in other nearby buildings. They often made their presence known by yowling for milk and snacks. Dad considered the cats to be partial barriers against the huge influx of mice and rats in the sheds and granary, or wherever we stored grain, so he never chased them away from those areas. Often the cats were so much out-of-doors and on their own that they were more feral than tame. But we kids enjoyed playing with the new litters of kittens when they arrived.

Another pack of animals—coyotes—were entirely unwanted. Under the front seat of Dad's pickup—and that of the family car as well—Dad kept a .30-30 rifle. If there was anything he hated, it was coyotes, so the rifles were at hand to take on those hated animals.

Dad was no different from other sheep ranchers. They all detested coyotes, the most threatening enemies of sheep in eastern Washington.

Coyotes were the most hated enemies at our sheep ranch. *1965-170.2. "Coyotes." Vardis Fisher Collection. Idaho State Archives.*

Over the years, our ranch became home to dozens, if not more, of wily coyotes. Dad's animosity toward coyotes remained— even escalated— each time he encountered ewe and lamb bodies torn apart by the ravenous predators. Over the years, packs of the vicious rascals barged their way onto our ranch—and often invaded our bands. Young lambs were particularly vulnerable to the attacking four-footers. And ewes, too, for that matter. Sometimes coyotes traveled in small packs but more often by themselves or with one companion. They would dash among the sheep, attack from the front, and try to bite into the throat of a ewe or the head of a lamb to bring them down. More often than not, the coyote ripped open the sheep's body, ate the entrails, and sucked up the blood, leaving most of the body uneaten. If the sheep sensed the presence of the killers, they turned tail and ran. When that happened, coyotes bit into their back leg, destroying a sheep's ability to move, before ripping open the body.

Dad tried several ways to keep the coyotes at bay. He stationed the herders and their dogs as close to the bands as possible. If an attack seemed imminent, herders sicced their dogs in that direction. But that defense/offense was dangerous, for if a fight ensued, the dogs rarely won, nearly always losing deadly battles. In coyote-infested areas, herders often carried rifles, hoping to bring down a coyote or scare them away with a loud shot. Dad also set traps around what seemed to be coyote burrows, but again there were dangers: dogs, sheep, or cattle might get caught in the traps. Even more dangerous, Dad and his herders tried to do away with coyotes by poisoning sheep carcasses and dragging them into known coyote areas. But that endangered the dogs who might wander onto the scene and eat the poisoned meat.

One other attempt to defeat the coyotes was more unusual. No binding love existed between sheep and goats. And the Etulains were not goat-lovers either, save for a few much-adored nannies like Annie. Like the biblical stories, goats were often separated from sheep. So, Dad built a goat pen, in which he kept dozens of goats. He included up to twenty or so goats with each sheep band and, true to their natures, the goats preferred to roam at the outer edge of the sheep band. If a billy goat sensed an oncoming coyote, he was much more likely than a ewe to turn toward the onrusher and take a defensive, even butting, stance. Dad was convinced that the obstreperous goats served as protectors, sometime saviors, of his sheep. He kept the goats, not for their milk or meat, but because they might serve as guards against the coyote invaders. Later, some Western sheepmen used llamas and alpacas for similar defensive reasons.

Dad retained his lifelong hatred of coyotes. He hid away several signs in the garage and often secreted one of the signs onto our back bumper. It read: "Eat more lamb, 10,000 coyotes can't be wrong."

Badgers were not the dangerous killers coyotes were, but they too were persona non grata on our ranch. These low-to-the-ground diggers opened up dangerous holes on the range that sometimes led to leg injuries for our horses and cattle. Often digging burrows in ravines, hillsides, and the open grasslands, badgers were fierce opponents once challenged by humans or other animals. Quite often, if a shovel was at hand, Dad filled in a badger hole with growing satisfaction. On other occasions he drove the pickup over the entry of the burrow, hoping to crush anything down below or to destroy the entryway. When we boys would see a badger, we went quickly in another direction. They had the combative personality of a midwestern wolverine, feisty creatures we wanted to avoid.

The Ranch was also alive with snakes. Thankfully, most of the rattlesnakes stayed away from the home place and resided near the rocky ridges, where they could sun themselves in warm weather. Bull snakes and garter snakes wiggled their way into our garden and even into the yards surrounding the house. We boys often played with the garter and bull snakes, capturing them in cans and boxes and continuously teasing them. Surprisingly, the bull snakes were rather slow and docile; that was unusual because we knew they could go after and defeat rattlesnakes.

Over near the same lake where many of our gophers resided, we also had a colony or two of what we called rock connies but which are more often referred to as hyrax or rock badgers. They were small, plump runabouts that seemed, in size and shape, a cross between a badger and a gopher. They lived in the rocks, loved to sun themselves, and seemed for the most part to be rather lazy. Our fun was in tossing rocks at them and seeing them scurry to their homes among the rocks. The plump little creatures also inhabited other nearby lakes and seemed more curiosities than dangers.

One of the strangest animals on the ranch was Cheechee the monkey. Mom, sensing our interest in monkeys (and perhaps her own too), answered an ad in the Spokane newspaper and purchased the small, young monkey for $75. Cheechee was a lively, half-tamed, and independent-minded creature. She often screeched her disagreements and frequently tried to run away, meaning we had to keep her on a chain or in a cage much of the time. We guys enjoyed showing her off at the Ritzville Adams County Fair. When she was more relaxed, she climbed on our shoulders or head, staying perched for a while. On

The most unusual animal on the ranch was Cheechee, our pet monkey. Here Dicky and Dan (holding Cheechee) attend a parade in Ritzville.

the downside, Cheechee, it was discovered, had a case of ringworm, and we boys soon had it in our hair. Trying to rub ointment on her ringworm outbreaks was like starting a civil war, leading to jumps, screeches, and attempted bites. One day, although on a chain, she got loose, and we could not find her. We speculated that she maybe got lost in the hog pen or caught her chain on something and could not wiggle loose. Cheechee the monkey was with us only for a short time.

Our ranch included other animals, but not many. We had a hog pen with several sows, piglets, and a boar or two, but these were for our meal table, not for market. We never had many chickens or turkeys, even though the Etulain family liked them for food. Dad thought chicken and turkey feathers might be chokers for our lambs if they tried to eat them, so we bought chicken and turkey from Safeway.

Interestingly, even though Dad raised hundreds—even thousands—of cattle and sheep, he never tried to raise crops for their food. Perhaps, if he had tried, it would have made his heavy workload too onerous, and maybe he did not want to try a part of ranching-farming about which he knew so little. Yet, owners of our ranch, before and after us, raised hay and other crops. And after we left The Ranch and moved to a smaller farm in Ellensburg, Dad became a thoroughgoing hay raiser, putting his sons to work mowing, raking, and bucking bales. But not at the Ritzville ranch. There, it was only sheep and cattle.

15

GAMES AND PRANKS

solated as we three Etulain boys were, we had to think up and organize our own games. True, we kept up with major league baseball, Spokane Indians baseball, the Washington State college teams, and the Sacramento baseball team in the Pacific Coast League, but these were distant activities, not something with which we were fully involved while living at The Ranch. When we did plan our sets of games, they often became combinations of games and pranks.

We played three-man baseball—up against the granary or the pump house as backstops. Ken did most of the pitching and Dan and I took turns trying to catch up with his fastballs. Since there was only one fielder besides the pitcher, we marked off an area—usually left or right field—as an acceptable site for hits. Sometimes we even ran the bases, using at-hand cow pies for our bases.

Other games were ones that were typical for young guys to play. Monopoly and marbles, for example. And we played a lot of Rook, an allowable card game because it didn't use the "playing cards" of the gamblers. (A bit later Ken was guilty of the grossest sin by sneaking into the house a deck of those evil cards.)

Our made-up games used stuff at hand. A small, two-wheeled cart (for delivering chopped hay to animals penned into the corral) became a wonderful go-cart zipping down a corral incline with

Most of the Etulain boys' games took place in the hay barns (on the left) and granary (on the right). We built forts and caves among the hay bales and played basketball in the granary. We considered the space in front of the granary to be our baseball stadium. In the winter, we skated or played on the ice that sometimes formed on a small lake located just on the other side of the fence.

all hands onboard. Most of the time we avoided breaking anything, including that which might need bandaging or crutches. The zipping only happened, of course, when Dad was out of sight.

Sometimes our games were more dangerous than we realized. We enjoyed going into the hay barns and climbing up to the top of the stacked bales of hay. We would then create our series of forts, tunnels, and traps. On more than one occasion we tumbled off the stacks and fell down on the fence posts placed at the bottom of the bale piles to keep the hay out of the dirt. In those falls, we could have been seriously injured. The Etulain luck kept us out of the hospital.

Another much-loved and frequently played game: rubber-gun fights. Probably this game started with Kenny, as most of our games did. We would first gather the needed parts. These included ¾-inch wide rubber bands or ringlets cut from a used inner tube. We tied a knot in the middle of these bands and then tied together several of the bands into a string. The string of bands was stretched along a stick, which was about a yard long and maybe an inch or less wide and about three to four inches top to bottom (this was our rifle barrel). Next, we nailed a piece of wood about 3" x 3" to the end of the stick next to the holder as our trigger place. Tied to the wood trigger piece was a clothespin, usually fastened very tightly by rubber bands. To finish the jerry-rigging, we placed one end of the string of ringlets over the far end of the barrel and stretched the string back to the close end and then into the clothespin, which we snapped tightly shut.

We faced several challenges in putting the rubber gun together. The string of ringlets had to be stretched as tight as possible because the velocity and range of our shooting depended on it. However, the ringlets could not be stretched too tight or they would pull out of the clothespin. And we couldn't use nearly rotten inner tubes; flawed ringlets would foul up everything.

The raucous and joyous gunfights sometimes went on for hours. Hiding around corners, peering out, and letting a brother or hired man's son have it—all on the sly.

Our fights were so lively and inviting that we even worked to modify our guns. On a few occasions, we instead constructed pistols, half the length of our rifles. More than a few times a shooter carried a rifle and a pistol—or, more unlikely, two pistols. Even more innovative, we built a rubber band "cannon." It was constructed from a 2 x 4–inch rail about 10–12 feet long, with a wheeled, box-like support placed on each end. We could wheel around our cannon in the deadliest of wars. A few times we raised up the cannon on the back end, held up its barrel end, and fired away at birds on the electric lines. Seems to me that on two or three occasions we actually hit a bird. No killings of course.

Our memories of the deadly rubber-gun fights were so long-lasting that many years later we introduced the backyard duels to our kids. They too enjoyed constructing the guns and then going after one another, cousin against cousin.

Near the family home was a good-sized lake rimmed with rocks on one side and more than a few gopher holes on the other side. We kids enjoyed "drowning out" the gophers, pouring gallons of water down their holes and chasing out the furry little creatures. The winner was the one who had baptized the most gophers that ran away.

Our frequent bicycle ridings often led to pranks. In these pranks, we destroyed the railroad agent's watermelons, swiped the herder's cigarettes, and enjoyed tossing rocks at hobos riding through The Ranch on freight trains. One Saturday we rode out to the paved road at The Ranch entry where county road workers had left their grader and other machines for the weekend. How we decided to let all the air out of the grader tires—or was it water—I don't remember. I do recall, however, my relapse in good thinking that night. Hoping to spare blame for myself, I guess, I told Mom, "Do you know what Kenny and Danny did today?" Of course, I wasn't planning to admit my part in the drama. But my two truth-telling brothers straightened out the facts, and Dad attempted to straighten out our next activities—with a sturdy, often-used switch.

Our neighbors were sometimes victims of our pranks—or just plain destructiveness. To the east of us was the ranch of two Basque brothers, John and Marcos Escure (Escujuri). Their ranch was twice as large as ours, sprawling over 20,000 acres, with more creeks and waterfalls, rocks, and meadows than our place. They too were sheepmen. Once in a while, Dad found reasons to visit the Escure ranch and talk shop on sheep matters. On one occasion when we boys went with Dad, we got tired of adult palavering and headed out to look around. Into the chicken coop we went. Seeing many unused eggs, we got into an egg fight, in which eggs and little unborn chicks were destroyed. We got tanned for that.

Sometimes we were victims rather than perpetrators of pranks. Once, while in St. Maries, we drove out to Uncle Juan's to visit. At first, he was not there. But all of a sudden, a large black bear came around the corner and came straight at us. Fear and pandemonium. Ken turned to look for a gun. To his credit, Uncle Juan didn't let us linger long in the fear. He threw off the large bearskin and greeted us. Much laughing followed, but not from the three skittish Etulain boys.

The herders, especially the dads among them, frequently teased us. Quite often when I would show up in the bunkhouse, especially after supper, the guys there would give me grief. On one wall, a series of sturdy hooks jutted out. One of the herders would grab me and place the back straps of my bibbed overalls over one of them. There I dangled—from the wall in midair—until the perpetrator or some other kindhearted dad took me down. I guess one of the boss's kids was especially fair game for such treatment.

Other pranks were unintentional—at least from us Etulain guys' point of view. When the sheepshearers came, they sometimes brought along a son or two about our age. One year one of those sons introduced us to his especially appealing BB gun. He vouched for the accuracy of the BBs but asserted they didn't do much damage. Ken decided to test the accuracy of the boasts. He talked Dan into packing the back end of his bibs with wool, so much so that he looked like a fat-tailed bear from the back. Dan walked away a few feet and slightly bent over, making the packed wool the target. Unfortunately, Ken's shot missed the wool, hitting Dan under the right shoulder blade. Ouch, ouch. He still feels it to this day.

A similar test came from the same BB gun guy. He fired the BB straight into the toe of his shoe, claiming afterward that he didn't feel a thing. Again, Ken wanted to test things. He grabbed the gun and fired into his own shoe, and wow, this time it really hurt. What Ken didn't know—and the shearer's son did not tell him—was that the shearer's son was wearing a pair of the famous steel-toed shoes that were so popular among loggers and railroad workers. Ken's blackened toe hurt for weeks.

Some of our pranks were more teasing than tricks. For example, once we began attending the Ritzville schools, the Adams family, with Mrs. Adams driving, came to our house each school-day morning to drive us about ten miles up the road to the waiting school bus. Among the Adams family was pretty, red-haired Eleanor. She was about Ken's age and classy; he fell for her. Boy did Dan and I have fun with that story, writing

Ken

+

Eleanor

everywhere, including on his notebooks. We even thought of writing the "love story" in our hymnbook on the page that listed the song, "In My Heart There Rings a Melody." Don't know what kept us from doing that. Obviously, Ken had the "hots" for Eleanor, although that was not the term that boys used in that time.

Sometimes in our little games we were guilty of blunders without really trying to play a game or pull a prank. Jutting up just west of the sheep corral was a rocky ridge with rollable boulders. We boys liked to see them bounce down to the base of the ridge. But the ridge was just behind the corral, so the jumping boulders could head dangerously in that direction. One day, busy with our rock rolling, we sent a particularly bouncy one down the side of the ridge. It had so much velocity and carryover that it bounced all the way to the wall of the corral and crashed through, causing a great deal of damage. Miraculously, we did not hit or kill any ewes or lambs.

Another of our fun games in warm weather was to go rafting on the large lake near our house, just behind the piggery. Pushing off the raft we had constructed, we poled our way around the deeper lake areas and pushed the raft in more shallow areas. We didn't think much, I guess, of swimming awfully close to the pigpen and where cows added their droppings. The pigs snorted around not too far from where we did our rafting and swimming. In one instance they were particularly rowdy penned-up pigs. Some of the mash prepared for them had fermented, and, after indulging themselves in their normal hoggish ways, they were drunk. Yep, plastered. They rolled around in their pen, squealing, and later rolled down to the lake's edge. It was a picture of piggish behavior forever etched in our minds.

16

THE END IS COMING

n the late 1930s, changes were in the air at the Etulain ranch. Shifting personnel and economic forces created flux.

New people came on the scene. In 1936, Mom and Kenny came to The Ranch as Dad's wife and new son. Then Dan (1937) and I (1938) joined the force. By the end of the 1930s, the Etulain family had reached its full number of five.

Economic shifts also reshaped The Ranch. During the second half of the 1930s, The Ranch profited financially. As Dad put it, "1936 to 1939 were big years, and we did well until 1942." But it didn't last. "The years after that were poor," he said. "Sometimes we didn't make a penny." He added, "It was hard to get good herders and without good herders I couldn't do well with sheep." Adding to the paucity of good herders, the federal government froze prices on lamb, mutton, and wool in 1942, but not on expenses. Feed costs were rising. Historian Alex McGregor succinctly summarized the up and down of the sheep business back then in one sentence: "The onset of World War II marked the beginning of the battle for [the] economic survival of the range sheep business." So while ranch profits increased at the start of the war, they precipitously decreased by its close.

Thinking he was losing in this battle, Dad decided in 1946 to sell the sheep and go into raising cattle. Here was Sebastian Etulain

When World War II brought down prices for mutton, lamb, and wool, Dad switched more and more to cattle raising. Here he is with a favorite Black Angus cow.

showing up again on his well-traveled path. If things did not work, try something different.

Major changes resulted from Dad's big decision in 1946. In switching to cattle raising, lambing, shearing, trailing, and herding nearly disappeared. The house and mountain property in and near St. Maries were sold. Now, a hired man was the central laborer on the emerging cattle ranch. Other workers were hired at roundups, branding, and marketing times. Spokane became more closely linked to the Etulain ranch, the location where we most often sold our fatted calves and yearlings and where we purchased heifer calves to raise as good stock for new moms in our own enlarging cattle herd. At other times, buyers would come directly to The Ranch to look over Dad's Hereford and Angus stock. The sheep corrals, by and large, stood empty; but the cattle corrals buzzed with new activity. No more docking; instead, branding in a heavily used cattle corral, branding chute, and loading dock.

Not everything instantly changed. Dad had owned a few cattle before selling his sheep. And he kept a few sheep while pushing into the cattle market. We kept the two herds of animals separate because cattle do not thrive in sheep-grazed areas.

Transitioning to a cattle ranch impacted the Etulain boys in several ways. Ken, especially. As a new teenager, he reveled in being a cowboy, prancing around aboard his spirited mount, Prince. Ken took part in roundups and often worked in the corrals moving cattle around. For Dan and me, the largest change was in fence building. The Adams County officials worked out a deal with Dad: if he would build new fences along the rerouted county road they were building through our ranch, they would gravel the road from that county road to our ranch house. So, we Etulain boys went to work, digging fence post holes and nailing barbed-wire and woven-wire fences to strings of cedar posts. Dad climbed on our sturdy Caterpillar tractor, hooked up the woven wire to the back of the Cat and stretched out the wire for dozens of yards. Our job was to quickly do the nailing on the wooden posts, many of which we had dug the holes for. Dad's superb handling of the Cat indicated how much he had learned in handling the machine largely foreign to him a bit earlier. He had purchased the Cat, brought it home on the back of his Chevy truck, and tried to unload it on a knoll near the milk house. Backing down off the truck, the untrusty machine got going faster than Dad liked. Yelling "Whoa" and pushing mightily on what he thought were brakes, he lost control of the Cat. It backed out of control down the knoll, smashed into the milk house, and destroyed our milk separator before coming to a halt.

Becoming more and more a cattle ranch called for other changes, especially in fence building. Dad never believed the wrongheaded idea that cattle and sheep could not coexist on the same ranch, but he did know that he needed to lay out his land in new ways. Part of the new layout involved erecting several extensive cross fences so he could move his cattle herds and sheep bands more expeditiously. He knew sheep might still find grass to feed on after cattle had been in an area, but he had to keep the animals separated and speed up their transfer from one ranch area to another. We boys were involved in helping build such cross fences when we left The Ranch in 1949.

Dad loved fencing. It appealed to him as especially good work for his sons. True to our Dad's tight-fisted nature, he gave us a dollar for the Ritzville Adams County Fair after we had spent most of a summer fencing. And told us to bring back the change.

Gradually, after selling most of the sheep and expanding his cattle holdings up to about 1,000 head, Dad began thinking about changing directions. He had done well financially but also had injured his back in lifting extra-heavy sheep. Maybe something else now.

The Higgins Real Estate firm in Spokane began coming to The Ranch to talk to Dad about other ownership possibilities. Gradually, the real estate men, Dad, and two other landowners put together a three-way deal. Dad would trade the livestock ranch for a 3,000-acre wheat ranch near Washtucna, which Clay Barr owned, and then Barr, in turn, would sell the Etulain ranch to the Fred Spencer family of Walla Walla. The Etulains and the Spencers would own new ranches, and Barr would take the cash. The size of the deal, worth nearly $1,000,000 in 1940, was big enough to hit the front-page headlines of the Spokane and Ritzville newspapers. Dad had purchased the McCall ranch in the early 1930s for roughly $4 per acre, and now he had traded it at a value of about $22-$23 per acre for the 8,800 deeded acres, or a total of nearly $200,000. Dad was always pleased with what he had accomplished in twenty years of ranch ownership.

17

AND THEN . . .

L ife on The Ranch in remote eastern Washington came to an end
for the Etulains in 1949. But the influences of The Ranch and
those people's lives shaped by The Ranch continued on. Some of
those influences were life-long; others needed revisions to fit changing
life situations.

AN ONWARD-MOVING DAD

Dad was convinced his life would change dramatically once he left
The Ranch. It did—and didn't. By the winter of 1949–50 he was
already back at it, making the transition to a different kind of ranch.
Near Ellensburg, 300 acres of irrigated crop and grazing land offered
a far different terrain and set of needs compared to his 10,000 acres
of sheep and cattle country. Still, Dad adopted some of his past and
embraced new things in adjusting to the Ellensburg farm just three
miles out of town.

He left the stock ranch and moved to this much smaller farm, he
told me much later, to "take it easy," maybe to even think of retiring—
at the age of forty-seven. But he wasn't going to let the new farm run in
the red, as the previous renter had. Dad had purchased the Ellensburg
place with a strong wool sale from The Ranch at the end of World War
II. Now he set out to make it turn a profit. He divided the farm/ranch

into thirds: one-third into sheep pasture, one-third into cattle pasture, and one-third into raising hay for the livestock. By the end of the next summer, he had all of these plans in place, and he had also learned to be an irrigator. Shovel in hand and accompanied by his doggie friend, "Old Maan," Dad set out every morning to check on the water and make sure the sheep and cattle were all right. At first, he was his own hired man, and then he tried to turn his sons into hay farmers.

Ken, Dan, and I soon learned how to mow, rake, and haul hay. Ken was the mower, Dan and I the rakers, and all of us hauled hay with Dad. Our father never wanted to be the hay baler, so he hired a neighbor to do that, but he certainly wanted his sons to pick up the bales in the fields and put them in the newly built hay barn. Speaking only for myself, I enjoyed "bucking bales," proving I was "becoming a man" in my early teens.

Alongside these changes, for Dad, was a string of continuities. He proved to be the never-stop worker in this new milieu as he had always been previously. He quickly joined and strongly supported the Nazarene Church in Ellensburg, and we all soon learned about the Safeway, drugstore, and hardware stores in Ellensburg. The town, although much more a cattle than a sheep town, was similar to Ritzville, just larger and older.

We stayed five years in Ellensburg. During that time, Dad enlarged and refined his work as a livestockman and hay grower. Interestingly, although he veered more and more toward raising and feed-lotting cattle, he never participated in the cattle organizations in Kittitas County. But he stayed aboard the sheep growers' county and state groups. Dad might have become more of a cattleman and hay grower, but he still identified with the sheepmen, as he would the rest of his life.

Dad and Mom did not enjoy the Ellensburg area. Primarily, I think, because of the very cold winters and late, late springs with their mighty and incessant winds. Maybe, too, cattle country was not their bag. As Dad put it, "we weren't happy in Ellensburg." Why, exactly, he or Mom never said.

The decision to move again came in the spring and early summer of 1954. Dad decided to trade the Ellensburg ranch for the medium-sized Maples Motel on the main street of Moses Lake. We had lived in eastern Washington, moved to central Washington, and were now back in the middle between Ritzville and Ellensburg.

Dad encountered another big occupational change in Moses Lake. Running a motel was something entirely new. He didn't like it, especially getting up in the middle of the night for latecomers. Dressed in work clothes and doing odd jobs, to many onlookers he seemed more the custodian than the owner.

Building a new home was daunting to Dad, so he put it off—for years. For several years Mom and Dad lived in little more than an expanded motel room; later, they occupied the office bedroom when they tore down old sections to expand the motel. Not until 1962, eight years after coming to Moses Lake, did Mom and Dad move into the brand new, dream-like brick house up on the hillside on Skyline Drive in Moses Lake. They enjoyed that spacious and solid home until their deaths in the 1980s and 1990s. In their wills, Dad and Mom gifted their home to the Nazarene Church to become the parsonage for their pastors.

Once in Moses Lake, Dad looked into new investment possibilities. That was also something pathbreaking for him. He purchased downtown property that he later sold to business builders. He also purchased other properties and built a series of two-story apartments, honoring Mom with the name Marilane Apartments.

While ensconced in Moses Lake, Dad did not stay homebound. For more than thirty years, he hung onto the 3,000-acre wheat ranch near Washtucna he had traded for in 1949. He did not know much about wheat ranching, but he kept the same man—Joe Huddle, an experienced wheat rancher—on the place for three decades. Dad made a couple of trips a year to see Joe, read the market reports on wheat sales in the local newspapers, and contact Joe if something came up. For all those years, the wheat ranch did well, and Dad used income from its wheat sales to build and invest in the Moses Lake area.

Revealingly, even though Dad was now a city man and would spend almost as much time in Moses Lake working as he had on his sheep ranch and farm, he retained his strong connections with lamb and wool people. He continued to serve on the county woolgrowers committee and helped with lamb sales. Even when he was in a wheelchair in his final years, Dad attended the woolgrowers' gatherings.

Dad also remained as active in Nazarene Church activities as he had for dozens of years previously. Sometimes he served as chairman of the church board, but because he hesitated to speak publicly due to his faulty English, he never gave board reports in front of the entire church. He had the reputation of being a more-than-generous giver of offerings. One fellow church member told an interesting story about Dad's donations. The church was planning a building expansion, and to raise funds it created something of a crossword puzzle display with dollar figures on each piece. The church member watched Dad, after the end of a Sunday morning service, begin to take down section after section of the giving puzzle. "I told him," she informed the family, "Brother Etulain, you've got to leave some pieces for the rest of us."

The good rumors about Dad's giving stretched even further. At a District Assembly gathering of Nazarene churches in eastern Washington, northern Idaho, and northeast Oregon, the district superintendent, who knew Dad well, told the crowd at an offering time: "Alright you folks, we need your help. And Brother Etulain, get out your billfold and help us." All this from the pulpit at the large gathering.

Conversely, Dad disliked the attention sometimes given to contributors. Popular in the Nazarene Church those days was a routine by which the pastor, trying to raise funds for a big or needy project, appeared before his congregation, and asked, "Who will give $100. . . or $50. . .or $10, please raise your hand." Dad detested such public display and never raised his hand to participate. Behind the scenes, however, he was more than generous.

An interesting trend occurred in Dad's final years. Although never a huge gambler, he took risks, like buying the McCall ranch, trading it for a wheat ranch, and becoming a motel owner and businessman in Moses Lake. But in his closing years, he returned to safer positions: he sold the wheat ranch to a Washtucna neighbor, sold the Marilane Apartments, and sold the properties he had purchased in Moses Lake. It was if he had taken his chances in the past, and now wanted to coast to the end on safer turf. He never expressed such feelings about retreating to safety, however. Perhaps Dad's backtracking was also influenced by the fact that none of his sons showed interest in joining their father in any investment or building projects.

Increasingly health-challenged in his final years, Dad suffered from a bad back that made walking difficult. Diabetes was another challenge. More and more he adopted a stay-at-home lifestyle, even though he tried to wobble or wheel himself out to his adored garden outback. Dad died at age 80 on 20 March 1983. The exact cause of his death was never given.

STAND-IN-THE-GAP MOM

Mary Lou Gillard Foster Etulain had been a supportive daughter and wifely woman of her times in her first and middle years. She continued to be so in the latter years of her life, but she also moved into leadership roles during her last decade or two.

Mom became more of a director of family traffic when we were in Ellensburg, particularly in decisions about the kids. Ken was in a rebellious stage because he never made a smooth transition in schooling from Ritzville to Ellensburg, and, growing increasingly discontent with what was happening in Ellensburg, he ran away from home. When he got into further trouble, Mom encouraged Ken's joining the service, which turned out to be a wise decision. At the same time, when Dan and I wanted to play sports, and Dad preferred our doing the chores, Mom helped work out a compromise where we could participate in one sport each year as long as we carried out our major chore, milking cows. Mom even drove us home after sports practices.

Mom also moved into another area where there were differences of opinion between Dad and her. When Mom's mother, Jennie Gillard, was no longer able to care for herself after a bad car accident, Mom took Grandma Gillard into our house. I don't think Dad wanted that to happen, but it did happen, following Mom's desire in the matter.

Clearly, too, Mom did not enjoy living in Ellensburg, and her distaste for that area helped them to make the decision to move to Moses Lake. Having some of her relatives living as farm families just outside town was probably a motivating factor for Mom to think of Moses Lake as better than Ellensburg.

Mom did not get all she wanted, however—certainly not as quickly as she wished. Over the years, as Dad gained more and more wealth, Mom dreamed more and more of a nicer home with substantial interior decoration. That dream was much delayed in Moses Lake. Imagine how she felt when it took nearly 10 years of living in small, enclosed motel rooms before that dream house was built. Through the years, one of Mom's recreational delights was drawing house plans with numerous rooms, comfortable bedrooms, a spreading living room, and a very modern kitchen. That dream was long in coming, and, even though Mom stopped drawing house plans after the new house was built, she added to, redecorated, and changed the dream house right up to her last days.

One of Mom's delights was the addition of three daughters-in-law to the Etulain family. Not everything went smoothly with them, however. While Ken was in the service stationed in Japan, he fell in love with a young Japanese woman, Noboko. Sad to say, the Etulain family, Mom included, did not want that marriage to happen and tried to stop it. Later, Mom changed her mind about the union and felt somewhat guilty when it ended. She made sure that the Etulains took care of the expenses when the now-divorced Noboko decided to attend business college in Spokane.

Later, when Ken remarried and Dan and I also married, Mom was the warmest of mothers-in-law. I never saw or heard her say anything negative about the three young women we brought into the family as wives and later mothers. She never showed any partiality in her treatment of them. It was a joy for Mom to finally have young women in the family.

As Dad's health declined, Mom almost single-handedly took care of him. Think of her pushing around his wheelchair, helping him in and out of bed, and, most challenging of all, getting him into and out of the bathtub. She obviously harmed her own health in trying to keep Dad going.

After Dad was gone, Mom was able to enjoy some things Dad had not relished as much as she. She loved to travel, and now she was able to do so. My wife and I took her to Hawaii, granddaughter Laurie went with her to Norway, and I traveled with her to England and Ireland for several days. Mom was interested in everything, but especially china and silverware shops. I ranged outside these shops while she ranged inside, for several hours. In England, she never got used to going to a pub, where evangelicals didn't usually enter, nor finding the feathers still on the chicken legs we were served. But when we got into an all-you-can-eat place, she loaded up her plate with enough for a week's feasting.

Mom's health began to fail after being afflicted with a malady something like Parkinson's disease. Eventually, she needed around-the-clock help. But before she died, she made sure that we sons, our wives, and the grandkids—all of us—were given more than generous inheritance gifts from Dad and her estate. Her death, at age eighty-five, occurred on 10 November 1999.

A REESTABLISHED BROTHER KEN

Ken's young life broke apart in our move from Ritzville to Ellensburg. In tight with Ritzville high schoolers, playing football and beginning to date, he lost all those close attachments in the move to Ellensburg during his junior year. Even before the first year was complete, he had dropped out of high school—in fact, he was asked either to attend classes or not come to school. And within the next two years, he had run away from home and tried the Nazarene College High in Idaho, which also ended in disaster. Then came the years in the Army. The stint in the service transformed Ken and led to his reestablishment with more than the family; he also transformed himself.

Ken served four years in the US Army during the Korean War, stationed largely in Japan. During that time he married Noboko, his Japanese wife. In these life-changing years, he seems to have lost his rebellion against the restraints of home and school. A new kind of direction and commitment surfaced.

Ken and Noboko returned to the United States and Ken, taking advantage of GI Bill support, enrolled at Central Washington College (later university) in Ellensburg. He pushed on to earn a BA degree in physics and math. He soon took jobs working for companies featuring sonar engineering. For thirty years of his career, Ken worked for the Edo Corporation, traveling around the world negotiating contracts with foreign countries. Unfortunately, early in these years, his marriage to Noboko disintegrated. We never learned exactly why, although a story circulated that Ken wanted children and Noboko did not.

Ken's life turnaround illustrates what some call "second chancers." These words refer to persons whose first time around did not work out well. But when a second opportunity came, they grabbed it—like one of Ken's earnest retrievers after an errant rabbit. Ken not only bounced back from family and school disappointments; he also did the same in his second marriage. His new wife, Julie, proved to be the warm-hearted, supportive, and amenable mate that he needed.

For as long as I can remember, Ken was drawn to animals. He seemed superglued to the memory of our McCall ranch. For Ken and his two younger brothers, that ranch brought about the deepest and strongest of attachments. It was our Harvard and Yale of the out-of-doors.

The animals of The Ranch as well as those in later years had a special fascination for Ken. There was the pet duck; Linda, the goat;

Tuffy, the dog; and Prince, the proud, prancing horse. Ken identified with The Ranch and these and other animals. They stirred his emotions throughout his life.

I saw more and more of our parents in Ken as he moved through life and on into retirement. As it did for Mom and Dad, family came first for Ken. His children—daughter Laurie and her husband, Gary; son Eric and his wife, Trista; and daughter Stephanie and her husband, Rob—and their children became important, attention-grabbing projects. Like our father, Ken also became a superb worker, one on whom trust, leadership, and onerous tasks were thrust. Like our mother, Ken had great hopes for his children, secretly and energetically working to ensure their futures.

And like our Mom and Dad, Ken relied on his mate. My wife, Joyce, tells me that the greatest thing Ken did was to bring Julie into our family. On these matters Joyce is always right. Julie was of great benefit and support for Ken—especially in providing home, hope, and solace while Ken traveled the world. Toward the end of his life, I once emailed Ken, saying how fortunate we were in our choice of wives. "Yep, you're right," he replied, and then added, "especially when they agree with us."

Sometimes Ken and I saw eye to eye and teamed up. We were lifetime Yankee fans, worshippers of the pinstripers. We labored like two evangelical preachers to convert our brother, Dan, to our sacred cause. He remained an unrepentant sinner, supporting first the rascal Cleveland Indians and next backsliding to the Seattle Mariners. Dan had the sacrilegious gall to adopt the attitude of "anybody but the Yankees." For other sports teams, however, Ken and I didn't agree. Try as I might, Ken never could be convinced that my then-beloved New Mexico Lobos (sited in the state where Joyce and I lived for 22 years) were just as or more worthy of loyalty than his Utes. Ah, well, not all seeds fall on fallow ground.

Ken tried to keep his love of animals alive in his later years. When living in Salt Lake City, he found a location that allowed space for horses, dogs, and other animals. In his last place of residence, Coalville, about an hour east of Salt Lake City, he developed a ranchette with other animals. A ranch and animals were in his blood.

In his retirement, Ken enjoyed family life, running a small ranch, collecting guns, and hunting with his son. Then the health challenges came. He fought them but died from lung cancer at age seventy on 10 April 2004.

NEAR-AT-HAND DAN

Dan and I followed similar paths for several years after leaving the big ranch. In Ellensburg we attended five years of junior high and high school, playing sports, learning to drive cars, and being attracted to pretty girls. We also learned to be farmers, helping primarily with Dad's hay growing, cutting, and baling and helping to tend sheep and milk cows. Between our junior and senior years, Mom and Dad moved to Moses Lake, where we completed a final year of high school. Again sports, cars, and church young-people gatherings were our main activities.

After thinking about other college possibilities, we both decided on Northwest Nazarene College (NNC; later it became a university) in Nampa, Idaho. That pleased Mom—that we were going to college and that we were going to NNC. Both of us ended up being on the five-year plan, Dan graduating in business and I in history and English. Cars and sports were part of those years too, yes, and especially girls. Dan found a mate in Kathie, a strong student from Boise; and I, Joyce, a dairy farmer's daughter from the Oregon coast.

Dan went directly into teaching. His first assignment was at a junior high in Boise, where he taught science. His classrooms became known for the animals in captivity and the numerous films he used for teaching.

Then again our careers overlapped. Dan decided to go to graduate school at the University of Oregon, where I had gone just weeks after finishing at NNC. For the next few years, Dan and Kathie and

Joyce and I were living not far from one another in Eugene, with our employed wives helping us to pay for our graduate school education.

Dan and I returned to home ground when we took positions at our alma mater, NNC. He taught a few courses and served as dean of men. But when a dissertation committee member would not accept Dan's dissertation, he did not complete his doctorate at Oregon. But typical of my two big brothers, Dan also became a "second chancer." He enrolled in another doctoral program at Northern Colorado University (University of Northern Colorado) in Greeley. When he completed his doctorate there, he took a job at Sheldon Jackson College in Sitka, Alaska.

Dan and Kathie and eventually their two sons, Todd and Troy, would "grow up" in Sitka. Arriving in 1972, Dan is still there after nearly fifty years of residence. At first, he taught courses and served administratively at Sheldon Jackson, and then he moved more and more out of the classroom. As the college gradually dwindled and stumbled toward closing, Dan began to expand on his previous audiovisual work as a public school and college teacher and professor. He became a television man, more and more involved with a television station in Sitka until he became its owner.

Some might think there were no signs of Dan's sheep ranch heritage in his new occupation in Sitka. Not entirely so. As recalled, Dan was already a toy man, a tinkerer with games, and intrigued with gadgets while still a boy. Science education and teaching built on those interests. And now his television work was building on these longtime backgrounds and experiences.

Another inheritance from a sheep ranch Dad is clear in Dan's pilgrimage. He has been persistent—better yet—consistently persistent. If something has not worked, try it again, or something slightly different. Month after month, we saw our dad continuing to move on, even if he had been temporarily stymied. I think, too, that now in his middle eighties, Dan embodies another Dad principle we learned way back, even though Dad may not have articulated it until later in life. It was this: when people spoke of retirement and sitting around, Dad said, "I can't think of living without working," and then out to his garden he would stumble. Or he would talk about getting to the next woolgrowers' roundup. Dan embodies that sheep-ranch heritage of perseverance right now.

In another way, Dan followed a long tradition that had begun at The Ranch. Like Dad and Mom, Dan remained a staunch Republican, as did Ken. Dad made clear his political partisanship on one occasion when he said, "I wish those communists over there in the western part of the state [Washington] weren't so much in control." He was referring to the Democratic Senators Henry "Scoop" Jackson and Warren Magnuson. Dad was strongly tied to US Rep. Hal Holmes, who stood for many of the values and positions of eastern Washington farmers and ranchers. Dan has continued the family's Republican heritage.

Dan and I traveled the same path in religious affiliation, one that stretched back to our first attendance in the Ritzville Nazarene Church. Like our Dad and Mom, we felt comfortable in that denomination, even though shifts in musical presentations sometimes set our teeth on edge.

MY OWN STORY

I told a friend recently that throughout most of my life, I've been a middle of the roader on most ideas and trends. Some of the middling path stretches back to The Ranch years; some more recent actions are breaks from that past.

Probably the strongest influence was my discovery of books. Books came to me in the little library at Lantz School, from my grandma via the book bargain bins (five to ten cents) of Churchill's Books in Yakima, from books like the Hardy Boys my mom bought during Spokane trips, and, most of all, from the Carnegie Library in Ritzville. Life at The Ranch was distant, isolated, and did not provide much conversation; so, reading became my most addictive recreation. I never found a cure for the addiction; it only got worse.

Engagement photograph of Dick Frulain and Joyce Oldenkamp in 1960; marriage followed in 1961.

But math was my main academic interest until my sophomore year at Northwest Nazarene College. In one of the many "just rights" in my life, a course in world literature taught by New Englander Marian Washburn introduced me to the joys of Homer, Chaucer, Shakespeare, and many other great authors. I learned there were classics other than the Hardy Boys, Nancy Drew, and sports stories. I was smitten and became an English major within the year. The other "just right" at NNC was history courses with Bob Woodward as instructor. He taught me how to think analytically, particularly in writing book reviews. That was a tough lesson, because previously truth had come to me through my parents, my church, and other adults. Now I was pushed to think for myself about books—their ideas and their strengths and limitations.

Another just right coming out of NNC was my meeting, courting, and marrying Joyce Oldenkamp of Tillamook, Oregon. When we began to get serious after a couple years of dating—we dated four years before marrying—I told Mom that Joyce was an ideal mate for me. She was quiet, soft, and easy to get along with; something an impatient, outspoken, and contrary half-breed-son-of-a-Basque needed. That proved to be true. Joyce became a wonderfully supportive wife, putting me through graduate school and serving as a loving mother to our daughter Jackie, as an all-star high school English and college speech teacher, and then for years as a first-rate librarian.

Within a few weeks after my graduation from NNC in early June 1960, I enrolled in a master's program in English at the University of Oregon in Eugene. Things did not go well during the first two terms. I was in over my head and got Cs in two classes, the equivalent of a failing grade in graduate school. (I had earned all As the past two years as an undergraduate.) I thought perhaps I could not do graduate work. But, gradually, I learned there were tricks to becoming an adequate-to-above-average graduate student. Getting up at six every morning, I worked for weeks on end in trying to write an analytical, evaluative seminar paper. It worked; I could see now how I had

Dick and Joyce gained their PhD and MA, respectively, in summer 1966. Joyce's parents (left side) and Mom and Dad (right side) all gathered at the University of Oregon in Eugene for graduation ceremonies.

surmounted one of the largest barriers to my becoming an acceptable graduate student. I also sensed I was out of step with the current trend in English departments in their fascination with the New Criticism, in opposition to my delight in literary history. Realizing that alienation in English graduate work, I transferred to the history department and pushed on to earn a doctorate in American history, with a minor in American literature and a dissertation on a Western historical novelist (Ernest Haycox). I learned in graduate school the truth of a cliché: hard work pays off.

One thing from my ranch heritage changed in 1964. I converted—my family might have said I backslid—to the Democrats. My father and mother and my two brothers remained rock-solid Republicans, but I changed largely because of the influences of my graduate school reading and teaching and because I came to believe in a strong central government that offers far-reaching social programs.

Dick while teaching at the University of New Mexico (1979–2001). He edited the *New Mexico Historical Review* (1979–85, 1991) and directed the Center for the American West (1989–2001).

Without much thinking on the matter, I quickly accepted a job at my alma mater, NNC, to teach in both the English and history departments. I enjoyed the experience and wished I could have had two careers, one spent entirely at NNC and the one that I followed at state universities. After two years of long hours of preparation and stimulating teaching at NNC, I decided like Henry James's hero in his novel *The American* that I had stayed too close to my family and church womb and needed new experiences. After one year on a teaching exchange and another postdoctoral year on the East Coast, I took a position at Idaho State University, where I stayed for nine years, 1970–79. Then, again thinking I needed a larger, more advanced graduate program in which to involve myself, I moved to the University of New Mexico (UNM), where I taught from 1979 until retirement in 2001.

My years at UNM were both "just right" and very stretching experiences. When I arrived in the fall of 1979 as editor of the *New Mexico Historical Review* and professor of history, UNM had the nation's largest contingent of American West historians. The geographical emphasis allowed me to build on my own Western experiences and training to teach a variety of Western history courses. It gave me the feeling that my own autobiography was being taught in some of my classes.

But I also felt overpowered by the backgrounds of many of my colleagues. Many were products of Ivy League, Big Ten, or other first-rate institutions like the University of California. I felt that my undergraduate work at "Jesus Tech" (Northwest Nazarene) and the University of Oregon did not measure up. So, again, following my dad's model, I would have to outwork them, to become something of a publication machine since I couldn't surpass my colleagues in brilliance and analytical talents. The desire to move ahead of the pack was a major impulse in my career at UNM—and beyond.

I also learned that I had stayed too close to my rural background in my teaching. My moment of epiphany came shortly after completing a lecture on the Populists in a US history survey course. I had indulged myself in talking about one of my favorite historical subjects, trying to raise students' sympathies for downtrodden farmers and ranchers of nearly a century earlier. After my lecture, a student approached me and bluntly asked: "Professor, why is it we get so much on farmers, ranchers, and other rural people in this course and so little about cities and the folks who live there?" His Eastern US accent betrayed him as alien to the American West, where I was teaching. But much more significantly, his question became, as I thought about it then and later, a turning point in my understanding of who I am and what kind of thinker and teacher I had become.

The illuminations from that moment were not all instantaneous, of course. Over time, I began thinking of how many facets of my teaching, my interpretive stances about history, and my choice of subjects in my specialty area of the American West were closely tied to my early years on a Western sheep ranch. Those early ruminations led to others about whether those ranch backgrounds unconsciously shaped more of my teaching and values than I realized. I began to ponder how much my family, especially my father and mother, had influenced my classroom teaching. In the years since the opening moment of that epiphany, I've been increasingly interested in examining the links, direct and indirect, between my ranching heritage and my career as professor of US history, particularly its Western history.

I began to see that blindnesses and oversights were fellow travelers in my excessive emphases on farmers and ranchers in American history. I didn't know much about cities, had never lived in a town of more than 50,000 for more than a few months, and was in my early forties before my family and I moved to a good-sized city, Albuquerque, New Mexico. That meant my boyhood and early adult experiences were primarily on ranches, farms, or in small cities. I had little personal identification with city dwellers, laborers, and urban immigrants.

My students were getting double doses of agricultural and rural history and too little urban, labor, and Eastern US immigrant history. Admittedly, the omitted subjects were not of great interest to me, but, worse, I was providing a slanted, inadequate treatment of US and Western history, largely because of the narrowness of my own experiences and interests.

Several new experiences gradually made me aware of the truncated, distorted views I was providing in my American history courses. The student who challenged me about the overly large emphasis on the Populists and the oversight of Eastern, urban topics was but one of these converging forces of change. Others came from new historical trends in my specialty field of Western history, and still others from my graduate students.

Until the 1960s, American frontier and Western history remained much in thrall of the ideas of Frederick Jackson Turner and his loyal followers. In the 1890s, Turner told his colleagues that the American frontier was more instrumental than European influences in shaping the course of US history. He was not urging his colleagues to forget transatlantic currents of thought and experience but encouraging American historians to pay more heed to the molding power of the frontier on American life and institutions. Less innovative and ana-lytical than their mentor, Turner's disciples took a much narrower approach to frontier history. The disciples were more orthodox than their leader.

Colleagues advocating for newer approaches to Western history, those that disagreed with Turner, wanted to move in other direc-tions. Undoubtedly much influenced by the yeasty 1960s, these new views began to emerge in the late 1960s and into the 1970s. Younger historians—and mid-career scholars—commenced to examine the major roles that racial and ethnic groups, women and families, and the environment played in the history of the American West. Many researchers also turned to studies of Western cities. Indeed, historians with a statistical bent were able to show that the region lying west of the North Dakota to Texas range of states was the most urban part of the United States, with California the most urban as well as the richest agricultural state.

These historiographical transformations greatly impacted my thinking. In addition, I was now teaching numerous masters and doctoral students and even offering a course that surveyed classic and recent interpretations of the American West. Reading and teaching these newer, broader interpretations of the West forced me to rethink my interpretive stances in my chosen field of specialty—and eventually to reexamine my own Western experiences.

An opportunity to put these newly understood interpretations came about in the mid-1980s as I began to coauthor a textbook of Western history. In preparing the sociocultural chapters of the book, I sketched out in broad outline the urban expansion of the West without overlooking the important rural, agricultural influences on the post-1900 West. Now, I could provide the balance between the rural and urban Wests missing in my earlier thinking and previous lectures and writings about the region.

Moving beyond this new balance, I also saw that I needed to add new ingredients to the story. No longer, for example, would it be a pioneer story largely about men but now also about farm and ranch wives, ethnic immigrants, minority workers and owners, and a post-1900 history. Ambivalent and agonizing passages about ranchers who overgrazed their pastures and used too many dangerous insecticides also worked their way into my narrative. And, after further foot dragging, I had to admit that some of my beloved Populists were blind to their own prejudices, unable to see that a few of their problems were self-inflicted.

In my middle-to-later years of teaching, I came to new understandings of Dad's shaping influences on my career. Dad was not a congratulator—at least not very often. On a few occasions he thanked Mom for her superb garlic-spiced roast lamb dinners and her top-notch cinnamon rolls. And I recall two or three times he saluted the good work of herders and ranch workers. And he had a few praises for ministers. But I don't remember his showing his pleasure with my graduating from college, marrying Joyce (whom Dad and Mom dearly liked), or gaining a doctorate in history. I do recall one surprising compliment, however. Mom and Dad were visiting us in Eugene when I got an unexpected call telling me I had passed the French exam needed for my doctoral degree. Dad was surprised and commended me for achieving that.

For a long time, I failed to understand that, although Dad did not

Dick delivering his presidential address before the Western History Association in 1999 in Portland, Oregon.

sing the praises of his sons or most others, he did live a life that modeled what we could achieve. I did not recognize that adoptable pattern until well after leaving home. When I did, I saw in Dad not a person who overflowed with praise for others but one whose humble path and determination had inspired me to overcome my own barriers. Dad arrived in 1921 without money, education, a clear job, or valuable connections. Despite these large deficits, he was, twenty years later, successful beyond dreams as a rancher, businessman, churchman, husband, and father. He had achieved these roles because of his due

diligence. He would, in his own words, "just have to outwork 'em"—
and he did in every way.

Dad's path became mine. When I faced barriers and even possible failures as a beginning graduate student, a new professor, and a
scholar, I adopted Dad's motto—"just have to outwork 'em." It was
not background nor brilliance but discipline and diligence that would
call the shots. Today I see and have accepted Dad's emulative footsteps.
It all came from my experience growing up at The Ranch and only
expanded as the years have unfolded.

Now, retired and a professor emeritus, I have the time—and interest—to ponder the connections between my personal experiences as a
ranch and farm son and my nearly forty years as a professor of Western
history. In my first years of teaching, I thought with my heart and
memories, in some ways illustrating the truism that "the unexamined
life is not worth living." New personal experiences and fresh research
in my specialty field showed me the inadequacy of drawing too heavily
and emotionally from my own experiences when offering a history of
the American West. I would retain the warm, encouraging memories
of my sheep ranch past but place them within a larger, more evaluative
story. My past took on new kinds of meaning. The sheepherder's son
on a remote Western ranch had become the resident of a larger, more
complex West.

18

BACK TO THE RANCH

The idea of a back-to-The-Ranch trip percolated in my mind for several years. Meanwhile, as noted in the prologue, I planned a family reunion to celebrate my mother's 80th birthday in 1994. Why not go further, I suddenly realized, and take our kids to The Ranch, the place they had heard so much about? I would plan the trip, inviting both Ken and Dan, their wives, and all the kids.

I decided to include the St. Maries summer sites, the home in town, and the mountain pastures near Calder and Herrick. So, we gathered at St. Maries and quickly visited the remembered spots. Heyburn Elementary School, the Handi Corner for lunch, and Main Street were the first stops.

When we arrived in town three years later, I curiously had difficulty locating our summer home. The intervening fifty years without revisits had dulled my memories. I even led us, at first, to the wrong house. But once I located it on another try, our arrival at the right house reopened the old neighborhood for me: the Osures across the street, Dr. Robins's house down at the corner, the Critzers across the alley, and Mrs. Green's down at the end of the alley.

Some things were gone. None of the residents of those homes, whom I had known as a boy, were still there. The Nazarene church we had attended had left its modest building and built a new, inviting church

The Etulain guys—Dick, Dan, and Ken—gathered in front of their favorite restaurant, the Handi Corner, on the main street of St. Maries. It was located about a half-dozen blocks from our house. Best ice cream in town.

across the water. The hospital where Dr. Robins took out our tonsils? Gone. But most things were at least located where they had been.

Next, off we went up the St. Joe River for thirty miles or so to Calder and Herrick. The tracks of the Milwaukee Road, so important to Dad for shipping his bands of sheep, were gone; we could even drive on the old railroad roadway. I noticed how much more Ken remembered about those locations and sights than Dan or I. Dan was seven and I six in our last summer in Idaho, but Ken was eleven, and he had traveled more to the mountains than we had. His stories gave the family the most information. The old cabin in Herrick was absent, and the creeks seemed almost unfamiliar. The loading and unloading pens in Herrick were gone with the disappearance of the Milwaukee. Tiny Calder struggled on, but Herrick had largely disappeared.

Traveling back to the Ritzville ranch from St. Maries, we decided to drive through some of the small Palouse country towns where Dad had trailed bands of sheep over the years. Neither Dan nor I could recall much about the towns. But some of the old attachment we had for those small towns resurfaced as we drove through them.

On to The Ranch. We drove down the paved country road bordering the northern edge of The Ranch, especially looking at the lay of the land and recalling what we had experienced there. Our kids and grandkids wondered about the dated—even decrepit—fencing and the rather barren, colorless pastures spreading beyond. Their comments set me to thinking: yep, it was an out-of-the-way place, and yet had clearly shaped and reshaped our lives. I began to ponder even more those shaping influences.

On to the home place, where Randy Spencer, the owner and son of the man who had bought The Ranch in 1949, met us for a chat in the backyard. We enjoyed talking to him about his family's use of the place as a cattle ranch compared to ours primarily as a sheep ranch. They grazed hundreds of cattle now, but also devoted small acreages to raising hay for feed. We soon noticed other changes. One of our childhood hangout spots, the Hole in the Ground, had become their dumping ground. They had also put up several cross fences (which Dad had planned to do) to better accommodate moving their cattle rather than allowing them to roam free-range. They had experienced tragedy, too, when a deformed-calf outbreak removed twenty percent of their baby beef. Evidently the cows had ingested a plant that led to the deformities. They shut down some of their operations because of the threat.

We retreated to Ritzville that evening, completing our ranch return. But like a historian looking at a pile of newly discovered research

The Etulain men—Dick, Ken, and Dan—meeting with Randy Spencer, then-owner of the former Etulain ranch, in August 1994. The view is looking out of the backyard of The Ranch home, showcasing the grasslands and scab rock in the distance.

The Etulain guys showing off the barbed-wire fences they helped to erect among The Ranch rocks.

materials, I began to think reflectively about my ranch experiences—now after nearly a half century.

I think the head-on, never-stop work pattern of my Dad influenced me most. Even though I turned away from ranch life, I inherited and put into action Dad's "just have to outwork 'em" ethic. I adopted that motto, first, to compete with academic colleagues I thought miles ahead of me in their intelligence and training. Later, that push drove me to try to out-publish those working in my field of Western history.

Pondering more of my ranch experiences, I realized how much I had enjoyed growing up with two energetic brothers. We played and pranked together. In those activities, I learned about working with others. At the same time, since nearly all my relationships on The Ranch were with other males, I gradually understood how little I knew about girls and women. They were strangers. Only Mom represented what a woman might be.

In The Ranch years, I also had begun a religious journey that I have followed the rest of my life. Dad and Mom lived out a dedicated and appealing evangelical lifestyle. Early on, I vowed I would become a Jesus follower and kept that vow. However, Dad's decision to become an evangelical and my conviction to traverse the same path separated me from Basque culture, since that cultural-ethnic group moved in directions quite different from those of evangelicals.

Finally, at The Ranch, Mom planted the deep, fertile seeds of schooling. She made sure I understood that higher education is the Holy Grail—something to chase and hold onto. When I expressed a delight in books and reading, Mom nourished that interest by buying books and making sure we got to the library. So did her mother, Grandma Gillard, who also brought me books. The seeds Mom planted lay dormant for nearly all of my public school education through high school; fascination with sports proved a barrier. But those dormant seeds were watered and fertilized nearly 10 years later in the college literature courses of Marian Washburn at Northwest Nazarene College. Her World, British, and American literature and English novel courses, linked with the wonderful American and English history courses of Bob Woodward, turned me into a bookie. And it was a joy for me and my wife, Joyce, to pass on the love of books to our daughter Jackie, who became, like her mother, a children's librarian. The fertile seeds for books had not only sprouted; they had blossomed into perennials. Bibliomania reigned.

So the major ranch legacies were Dad's drive, brotherly hangouts, religious joys, and a love of books instilled by my mom. Inheritances from The Ranch years. Those gifts still stretch my mind while they warm my heart with memories.

SOURCES

D
ad did not keep records of his more than a half-century as a
sheepherder and rancher. A recently surfaced journal (of scattered tax and loan records), however, provides some financial
facts and personnel information, the latter including names of a few
men who worked at The Ranch. The most embarrassing information
the journal shares is about me—that this writerly son had to borrow
money to get married, to go on his honeymoon, and to purchase a
mobile home for his first house. Not until the 1960s, when US interest
in ethnic and racial backgrounds started booming, did I talk directly
and extensively with Dad about his Old World backgrounds, his
early work as a herder in the Yakima area, and his later experience as
a ranch owner.

The sources mentioned here include only those that played a large
part in helping me to write this book. Their full citation appears in
the bibliography that follows.

For the lay of the land in eastern Washington, I relied heavily on D.
W. Meinig's superb cultural geography, *The Great Columbia Plain: A
Historical Geography, 1805–1910* (1968). Meinig briefly discusses the
Lake Missoula flood and Channeled Scablands that resulted, but much
more extensively examines how newcomers reacted to the terrain and
tried to mold it to their desires.

The best source, by far, in dealing with Old World Basques and
their entries into the New World is William A. Douglass and Jon
Bilbao, *Amerikanuak: Basques in the New World* (1975). Nearly fifty
years after its publication, this extensive account provides the needed
basic information on numerous Basque subjects, including their roles

as much-desired sheepherders in the American West. I also made use of the collected essays in Richard W. Etulain, ed., *Basques of the Pacific Northwest* (1991), particularly those about my father and early Basque immigration into the Pacific Northwest.

A model work on a major sheep business in the Pacific Northwest is Alexander Campbell McGregor's *Counting Sheep: From Open Range to Agribusiness on the Columbia Plateau* (1989). Although McGregor focuses primarily on his own family's experiences, he also furnishes valuable contextual information about other sheepmen, ranchers, and herders in the Pacific Northwest. *This Was Sheep Ranching: Yesterday and Today* (1976), by Virginia Paul, overflows with revealing photographs, but also includes helpful general background information on US sheep ranching. A similar book that focuses on Basque herders and also includes numerous illuminating photographs is *Basque Sheepherders of the American West: A Photographic Documentary* (1985), by Richard H. Lane (photographs) and William A. Douglass (text).

I found Steve Turner's strong narrative history of Ritzville and Adams County, Washington, *Amber Waves and Undertow: Peril, Hope, Sweat, and Downright Nonchalance in Dry Wheat Country* (2009), an entrancing work. Although the book deals primarily with wheat farmers, it also provides sparkling descriptions of other ranchers and of the town of Ritzville.

For general trends in the history of the American West, I relied on Richard W. Etulain, *Beyond the Missouri: The Story of the American West* (2006).

Those who wish a handy listing of the major books and essays on sheep and sheepmen in the American West should consult Richard W. Etulain, *Sheep and Sheepmen of the American West: A Bibliography* (2001).

BIBLIOGRAPHY

BOOKS

Douglass, William A., and Jon Bilbao. *Amerikanuak: Basques in the New World*. Reno: University of Nevada Press, 1975.

Drumheller, Dan. *"Uncle Dan" Drumheller Tells Thrills of Western Trails in 1854*. Spokane: Inland American Printers, 1925.

Etulain, Margaret Westin. *The J. M. Etulain Family*. Undated, unpublished manuscript.

Etulain, Richard W. *Basques of the Pacific Northwest*. Pocatello: Idaho State University Press, 1991.

_____. *Beyond the Missouri: The Story of the American West*. Albuquerque: University of New Mexico Press, 2006.

_____. *Sheep and Sheepmen of the American West: A Bibliography*. Albuquerque: Center for the American West, 2001.

Lane, Richard H., and William A. Douglass. *Basque Sheepherders of the American West: A Photographic Documentary*. Reno: University of Nevada Press, 1985.

McDermott, Paul D., Ronald E. Grim, and Philip Mobley (ed.). *The Mullan Road: Carving a Passage through the Frontier Northwest, 1859–62*. Missoula, MT: Mountain Press, 2015.

McGregor, Alexander Campbell. *Counting Sheep: From Open Range to Agribusiness on the Columbia Plateau*. Seattle: University of Washington Press, 1989.

Meinig, D. W. *The Great Columbia Plain: A Historical Geography, 1805–1910*. Seattle: University of Washington Press, 1968.

Padgett, W. Keith. *The History of Adams County*. Ritzville, WA: Adams County Historical Society, 1986.

Paul, Virginia. *This Was Sheep Ranching: Yesterday and Today*. Seattle: Superior Publishing, 1976.

Towne, Charles Wayland, and Edward Norris Wentworth. *Shepherd's Empire*. Norman: University of Oklahoma Press, 1945.

Turner, Steve. *Amber Waves and Undertow: Peril, Hope, Sweat, and Downright Nonchalance in Dry Wheat Country*. Norman: University of Oklahoma Press, 2009.

Wentworth, Edward Norris. *America's Sheep Trails: History, Personalities*. Ames: Iowa State College Press, 1948.

Zubiri, Nancy. *A Travel Guide to Basque America: Families, Feasts, and Festivals*. Reno: University of Nevada Press, 1998.

ESSAYS

Briggs, Harold E. "The Early Development of Sheep Ranching in the Northwest." *Agricultural History* 11 (July 1937): 161–80.

Bretz, J. Harlen. "The Channeled Scablands of Eastern Washington." *Geographical Review* 18 (July 1928): 446‑61.

―――――――――. "The Channeled Scablands of the Columbia Plateau." *Journal of Geology* 31 (November-December 1923): 617‑49.

DeRuwe, Milan (with John Ellingson). "Sheep Raising in Eastern Washington: A Reminiscence by Milan DeRuwe." Essay 8971. HistoryLink.org. April 2009. https://www.historylink.org/File/8971.

Douglass, William A. "The Vanishing Basque Sheepherder." *American West* 17 (July-August 1980): 30–31, 59–61.

Etulain, Dan [*sic* Richard W. Etulain]. "A Basque from Spain Becomes a Key Layman at Moses Lake: Sebastian Etulain." In *Architects of the Enduring: Uncommon Stories from Everyday Nazarenes*, edited by Neil B. Wiseman and L. Wayne Sears, 89–91. Kansas City, MO: Beacon Hill Press, 2001.

Etulain, Richard W. "Basque Beginnings in the Pacific Northwest." *Idaho Yesterdays* 18 (Spring 1979): 26–32.

―――――――――. "The Basques of Yakima, Washington." *Basque*

Studies Program Newsletter (Reno) 10 (May 1974): 3, 8.

————————. "Sebastian Etulain, Livestockman of the Northwest." In *Basques of the Pacific Northwest*, edited by Richard W. Etulain, 51–55. Pocatello: Idaho State University Press, 1991.

Laxalt, Robert. "Basque Sheepherders: Lonely Sentinels of the American West." *National Geographic* 129 (June 1966): 870–88.

Rousso, Nick. "Sheep Farming in Washington." Essay 21012. HistoryLink.org. May 2020. https://www.historylink.org/file/21012.

Shaw, R. M. "Range Sheep Industry in Kittitas County, Washington." *Pacific Northwest Quarterly* 33 (April 1942): 153–70.

INDEX

ABOUT THE AUTHOR

Richard **W. Etulain** is a professor emeritus of history at the University of New Mexico. He was the 38th president of the Western Historical Association in 1998-1999 and also president of the Western Literature Association in 1979. He is the former director of the Center for the American West at UNM, now the Center for the Southwest.

Etulain was born 26 August 1938 in Wapato, Washington. He majored in English and history at Northwest Nazarene College (1955-1960). He received an MA (1962) in American literature and a PhD (1966) in American history and literature from the University of Oregon.

Etulain has written or edited more than 60 books. They include *Conversations with Wallace Stegner* (1983), *Re-imagining the Modern American West: A Century of Fiction, History, and Art* (1996), *Beyond the Missouri: The Story of the American West* (2006), *The American West: A Modern History, 1900 to the Present* (with Michael P. Malone, 2nd ed., 2007). More recently he has focused on Abraham Lincoln and his links with the American West in several books.

Etulain has written two books on Calamity Jane and two on Billy the Kid. His literary history of the Pacific Northwest is forthcoming, and he is at work on a book on Basques of the American West.

Etulain lives with his wife Joyce, a retired librarian, in Portland, Oregon. They have a daughter, Jackie, son-in-law David, and grandson Adam nearby in Portland.